D1062671

Browning

BROWNING
BACKGROUND AND CONFLICT

F. R. G. Duckworth

with a Prefatory Word

by

WILLIAM LYON PHELPS

NEW YORK

E. P. DUTTON & CO., INC.

FIRST EDITION

To

L. R. F.

Χάλκεα χρυσείων

Prefatory Word to the American Edition

By WILLIAM LYON PHELPS

A S the poetry of Browning was popular in the
United States before it received anything like
its due recognition in England, so it is true today
that Browning has more enthusiastic readers and
certainly more students in America than in Great
Britain. He is studied by thousands of university
undergraduates and boys and girls in the secondary
schools.

A year ago I asked members of my class in
Browning at Yale to bring to me any allusions to
him or his works that they ran across in contemporary newspapers, magazines, and books; in two or
three weeks I had to announce a moratorium, as I
was flooded by the material they brought in.

Virginia Woolf, in an amusing article on Mrs.
Browning's *Aurora Leigh,* intimates that owing
to the popularity of Rudolf Besier's play, *The
Barretts of Wimpole Street,* which is at this moment in its prosperous second year at the theatres
in both London and New York, many more people
are now familiar with the individuals Robert and
Elizabeth Browning than they are with Browning's
poetry. Well, in America there are hundreds of
thousands of readers of Browning who have not
yet had the opportunity to travel to New York,
and successfully invade the Empire Theatre.

3

Mr. Duckworth's book is a serious, thoughtful, original study of Browning's genius, of his methods of composition, of his aims and ideals, of the growth of his reputation, of the peculiar appeal he made to men and women during the various decades of the nineteenth century. It is also an impartial and dispassionate examination into the kind of significance his poetry may have for us today.

With reference to the secondary title, *Background and Conflict,* which expresses not only the thesis of this work, but the reasons that induced Mr. Duckworth to write it, I prefer to make no comment, because I wish readers to reflect upon this themselves, without any previous suggestion. As to the source of Browning's poem *Christmas Eve,* which I pointed out in *Modern Language Notes* some twenty years ago, my belief in its relation to Browning's "orthodoxy" is somewhat different from that expressed by Mr. Duckworth.

Here at all events is a new book on Browning, bristling with ideas.

Yale University
11 November, 1931.

CONTENTS

INTRODUCTION

FOR nearly seventy years men quarrelled fiercely over Browning's poetry. Even to-day, a century after the publication of *Pauline*, though the flames of controversy have died down, the embers are still warm. Not many poets have been so violently quarrelled over for so long. There must be in his verse something more than usually vital, something, that is, more than usually capable of arousing a live interest in widely varying conditions of thought and taste.

When I considered this, it seemed to me a task worth embarking upon to inquire more particularly what kind of interest was in fact aroused by Browning in strongly contrasted situations. I selected for the purpose three periods, namely, the years 1850–59, 1890–99 and 1920–29, and searched out what had been said of him in each of these. The results are embodied in the first part of the present book.

The general level of criticism in these three decades varies in point of intelligence and insight. The reviews and articles published during the Fifties are nearly always stupid and often ill-natured as well, and it might not have been worth paying attention to them but for the following reason. After carefully examining the critical attitudes of the Fifties and the Nineties, I was struck by this, that in each decade the critics had tended, in different degrees, to be blind to those very qualities in Browning's poetry on which they might have been

7

expected to dwell with the most insistence. Whether
the same tendency exhibited itself also in the decade
1920–29 it was less easy to say for certain, but on the
whole there appeared to be a fair amount of evidence
that it was .so. On grounds of completeness,
then, and of contrast, it seemed that the inclusion
of the decade 1850–59 was justified, even though the
standard of criticism at that time was so low.

The decade 1920–29 was so engrossed with the
fact that Browning was in many ways a typical
Victorian poet that it had little thought to spare for
anything but his Victorianisms. And yet there
appeared to be in this poet's life and work a problem
which of all others might have been expected most
to interest this age, because it is a psychological
problem arising out of a conflict in his personality
and his poetry. It is with this conflict that the
second part of this book is concerned.

Such is the main aim of the present book. If by
the way it should suggest to some readers that
Browning in his person and in his poetry was more
interesting than they had realised, or that, although
he is generally considered in our own day to be a
Victorian of the Victorians, there are in his work
certain elements of a surprising modernity—that
will be all to the good. But to evaluate Browning's
poetry, to show how he stands related to other poets
before or after him, falling short of them in this,
completing or forwarding them in that—or, still
more inspiring and more difficult, to make us understand and feel how there throbs in his work, full
here and more feeble there, the authentic and eternal
rhythm of life, that is a task to which I have not
dared to aspire in this book.

                                              F. R. G. D.

PART I

BACKGROUND

CHAPTER I

THE POINT AT ISSUE

NOT a vast amount of humour is to be extracted from the Papers of the Browning Society of London, but one passage at least, occurring in the minutes of the twenty-second meeting of the Society, may still raise a smile. There it is recorded that, after a paper on " Some Prominent Points in Browning's Teaching " by Mr. W. A. Raleigh of University College had been read to the Society, the subject was thrown open to discussion. Thereupon arose one of the members, who suggested that the Society would obtain far greater benefit " if they left off discussing and went home and read their Browning." That member of the Browning Society was a certain Mr. G. B. Shaw.

On a first impulse one might say that no wiser advice was ever offered to the Society. But as one thinks over the matter a little further and perhaps more charitably, another reflection comes—how exceedingly difficult it was for the Society to read their Browning. And then again—not only for the Society but for anyone, in this day just as much as in that. It is not so much that Browning is obscure by reason of his language and his involutions of thought. Indeed, it is not only Browning who is difficult to read : it is every poet and every writer.

For, what happens to us, when we go home and try to read our Browning ? What exactly have we in mind when we speak of reading a poem ? Much,

obviously, beyond the mere deciphering of words.
Thoughts and emotions are conveyed to us, we say,
and the sum of these constitutes the poem's meaning
or message or signal. In much of what is said or
written about poetry it is assumed that this meaning
is one and definite. Given two readers equal in intelligence and, roughly speaking, alike in upbringing,
the poem, we think, ought to have very much the
same effect upon both of them—should produce in
both the same set of thoughts and emotions. It is
because of this assumption that men are angry with
those contemporaries of great poets who did not
understand and value them as we do. We think
that those contemporaries were perversely and wilfully blind, that they took no trouble to open their
eyes and their ears. If they had been honest and
persistent, they would have seen, heard and felt
the same things as we who read the poet now.

But what if our assumption is not justified ?
Notice that, if we are pressed, we shall admit easily
enough that readers, though they may be equal in
intelligence, may differ in other ways—in degree of
sensibility, for instance. Again, in the particular
mental images evoked by a poem there will certainly
be variations. " Et rose elle a vécu ce que vivent
les roses "—when you read this, do you see white
roses or red ? All these differences, however, may
appear to be relatively unimportant and quite
insufficient to account for the perversity of perverse
critics or to justify the members of the Browning
Society in continuing their discussions.

But once any man has sat down with a trusted
friend to compare notes honestly and candidly about
any one poem which each has read independently—
particularly if it be about some new or some un-

known poem whose author's reputation has not yet been appraised and fixed—then he will never again be able to feel so sure that all men of equal intelligence and like nurture must have moved in them the same thoughts and passions by the same poem. If it is for any reason difficult to test the truth of the statement, then recourse may be had to a book which has recently aroused much attention—Mr. I. A. Richards's *Practical Criticism*—in which many such experiments are described. And here and now an experiment carried out by the present writer somewhat on the same lines as those followed by Mr. I. A. Richards may be alluded to quite briefly. The persons who collaborated were not undergraduates (like Mr. Richards's collaborators), but mature persons. They were asked to read Browning's poem *The Flower's Name* (the first of the *Garden Fancies*)—but the title and the name of the author were withheld. After reading this, the next step was not to write a general appreciation of the poem, but to answer certain definite questions.

Of the forty persons who took part in this, thirty-five either had not read or forgot that they had read the poem. All of them were fairly familiar with Browning's better-known work, and all except one took pleasure in his poetry. They were men and women who in general terms would be called highly educated, and they could safely be taken as representative of an intelligent poetry-reading public. In recording their impressions they were entirely sincere and candid.

This is not the place in which to give a fully detailed account of the results of the investigation, but in summary form a very few of the more striking differences of impression may be recorded. Most of

the readers described the mood of the poem as
sentimental : to some of these the sentimentality
seemed gentle and inoffensive, to others it was
wholly nauseating. Some interpreted the poem as
the expression of a triumphant certainty, a cry of
exultation ; another group saw in it doubt and a kind
of wistfulness. Again, of the many who remarked
that it was a half-told tale, there were those who
complained that the picture presented was shadowy
and unsatisfactory—that the poet was negligent or
uncertain of his aim, while others judged that the
poem achieved a desired effect by means of suggestion.

Mr. Richards was not, of course, the first to observe the differences of impression and of judgment
formed by men of about the same intelligence and
nurture concerning one and the same poem, but
he has been the first to study those differences
seriously and systematically, to suggest a method of
measuring them, as it were, and of explaining them
by referring them to their causes. He himself, no
doubt, and others with him and after him, will carry
on to a further stage this investigation into the
differences of judgment of individuals. But his
work in this field suggests the existence of yet
another field of inquiry—a study of the differences
between characteristic opinions concerning a poet's
work formed, not by individuals in one and the same
moment of time, but by groups of men in different
ages. True, such differences have already formed
the object of study, in connection with Shakespeare
or Milton, for example. To come a little nearer
home to the subject of the present study, the changes
in men's attitudes towards Tennyson are noted in
Gwynne's well-known and widely read *Tennyson : a*

Critical Study. But a systematic attempt to seek for the explanation of these changes in the temper and the circumstances of the period in which each was formed does not appear to have been made.

Here a possible objection must be met. It may be argued that if fundamental differences are to be remarked in the judgments of individuals composing a group, it will be difficult to believe in the existence of a group judgment. And of a small group, of a group, for instance, of forty readers, such as that which read *The Flower's Name*, the objection must hold good. With very large numbers the case is quite different. Certain opinions and attitudes must then repeat themselves even in regard to one and the same poem. When not one poem is in question, but the significance and value of the whole of a poet's work or of a large portion of that work, the groups holding a similar opinion may be very large. To take a crude illustration, the two groups into which one might divide those who love Hardy's novels and those who hate them are obviously very large in comparison with the two groups of those who are drawn to him on account of his pessimism and of those who like him in spite of his pessimism.

To come now to the particular poet with whom this present study is concerned, everyone who has read him intelligently knows well that, after being neglected or held up to ridicule for the obscurity and harshness of his verse, he was later recognised as a supremely great poet, fitly to be named in the same breath with Shakespeare, while in our own day he has fallen from that high estate to the second class, as it were, and is esteemed one who, sometimes and within his class a supreme artist, can no longer be ranked with Shakespeare or even with Wordsworth in the whole hierarchy of poets. But in all the very considerable literature which has sprung up around his name, no book is known to the present writer in which an attempt has been made to study some of the typical differences of judgment with a view to classifying them and referring them to their causes. Such an attempt is now to be made.

It is not intended to write a complete history, as it were, of the criticism of Browning. The study will be carried on within narrow limits. Three periods, or moments of time, have been chosen out, namely, the three decades 1850–59, 1890–99 and 1920–29. They have been selected, not so much because in each of them any one phase or stage of development in the criticism of Browning came by its completest or clearest or most characteristic expression. If that had been the main consideration, it would have been impossible to omit the period in which Walter Bagehot produced his essay on *Wordsworth, Tennyson and Browning*, or the years which saw the publication of works by G. K. Chesterton, Stopford Brooke and C. H. Herford.

The reasons for selecting the three periods named were these. In the first place, the three decades are widely different from each other in general characteristics. Secondly, they are widely different in respect of the esteem in which each of them held Browning's work. The decade of the Fifties is on the whole inimical to the poet, although with the publication of *Men and Women* in 1855 he reached what has come to be regarded by common consent as the highest point of his achievement. In the decade following upon his death, the Nineties, his reputation came to its zenith ; also this decade may be regarded as marking the close of the Victorian

period of poetry.   Finally, in the Nineteen-twenties
those who cared for poetry and took note how it
grows and moves, seemed to become aware that a
new stage in the history of poetry had opened ; also
they felt (even those of them who had not succumbed
to the wave of anti-Victorian prejudice) that Browning might now be considered *rangé*.   And his rank
was to be that of Matthew Arnold, Swinburne,
Rossetti—quite definitely a rank below the very
greatest masters.

Two further ways in which the study is limited
must be mentioned quite briefly.   Although, as has
already been said, the different attitudes taken up
towards Browning's work in each decade will be
classified in some sort and the causes of them
suggested, a complete analysis of the causes would be
a task quite beyond the present writer's capacities.
Since the influences at work in any moment to
mould the judgments formed by a group of men are
elusive and innumerable, attention will in each age
be paid chiefly but not exclusively to the general
tendencies of poetic thought—that is, the thought of
poets and of critics of poetry.   And lastly, the inquiry will relate exclusively to the poet's English
critics (with the exception of Professor Irving
Babbitt).

CHAPTER II

THE EIGHTEEN-FIFTIES

THE Fifties and Sixties were, it is generally assumed, the golden years of the Victorian era. " Victorian " is a word rather too easily and loosely used by critics of our own day, and many of the criticisms directed against the age could very easily be robbed of their sting merely by asking critics to define and justify their terms. The Victorian age has come to be associated in most people's thoughts with much that has been picked up from reading Dickens, Thackeray, George Eliot, Trollope, and from the illustrated journals of the time. We are apt to find ridiculous, or ugly, or both, its antimacassars, its horsehair and mahogany, its houses without bathrooms, its crinolines and its whiskers. Much more serious imputations are mental stuffiness, prudery, hypocrisy, a wilful blindness to devastating evils, a sort of moral insensibility. Standards of taste ranged low in a time that produced the Crystal Palace.

It is not necessary to fill more detail into the picture, nor need we here delay to ask whether the picture is fair. It would not even have been necessary to sketch it on this page if it were not that this is the background against which many of the present generation are accustomed to place the poetry of Tennyson and of Browning. Anyone who has not yet passed his thirtieth year and has seen in a theatre or a music hall actors in Victorian dress dancing the polka has only then to be told that Tennyson of set purpose gave a polka rhythm to " Come into the garden, Maud . . ." for those lyrics to be at once and perhaps for always associated in his mind with something ridiculous and ungraceful.

- This Victorian England was economically prosperous, and, so far as one may generalise on such a point, it believed in itself and believed that its achievements marked an immense progress upon anything known to past ages, and that this progress would continue irresistibly through the future. The tendency to materialistic standards in morals, art and religion is undeniable. Not that this attitude was universal. It was not everyone who believed that all was for the best in the Fifties. Although the Oxford movement had flickered out, leaving the Church almost unsinged, yet trouble was breeding among those many educated people who were acquainted with the speculations of Strauss and Renan. And though *The Origin of Species* was not published until 1859, yet *In Memoriam* bears witness of the doubts and fears to which, in many minds, Robert Chambers's *Vestiges of Creation* had given rise. In his preface to the 1853 volume of his poems, Matthew Arnold speaks of " the bewildering confusion of our times," and implies that the age was one of " spiritual discomfort." But though some few of the clearer-sighted were startled and alarmed by what they saw and read, it is clear that the majority of Englishmen were ready to be angered with any writer who depreciated the material prosperity of the time or cast its progress in doubt. In their view, the man of letters must accept it as his mission to forward the general deed of the time and to preach the doctrine according to Bentham.

Now let us ask what attitude the reading public of that day might be expected to take up towards Browning's poetry. Can any signs be discerned which might lead one to expect a favourable reception?

A few such signs there are. In the first place, there was being produced in this decade a mass of literature which has since vindicated its claim to greatness. And these works were enjoying considerable success, judging by the bookseller's balance sheets. In particular the fortunes of Tennyson might seem to justify bright hopes on Browning's account. For Tennyson, who had struck a new note in poetry and had previously been subjected to a stinging rebuke from the *Quarterly*, had now, with the publication of *In Memoriam*, established himself in popular favour. It is worth recalling that other successes of the decade were *David Copperfield*, *The Newcomes*, *Adam Bede*. Then again, not only had the literary reviews shown themselves favourably disposed towards Tennyson, Dickens, George Eliot, the Brontës, but also one can find in this or that number general critical pronouncements of such a sort as to suggest that a new writer might expect fair and judicious treatment. One reviewer expects poetry to enlarge its province and to become conversant with " whatsoever stands immediately and obviously in relation to universal truths and permanent humanity." Another shows that he is struggling to free himself from his own prejudices. For having said that *Lohengrin* reminded him of the wind whistling through the keyholes of a cathedral, he makes haste to add that this was merely a personal impression and to remind himself of the titters with which critics had greeted the first performance of a Beethoven symphony at a Philharmonic concert.

But any hopes based upon such evidence of enlightened critical opinion would surely be illusory. The evidence is very slight, and even if there were none on the other side, no one could feel happy about Browning's chances of recognition, when he recalled the general tone and temper of that day. He might for instance ask himself—" If Tennyson was at that time recognised, on what grounds was that recognition accorded ? Perhaps Tennyson succeeded in spite of his better qualities ? " As it happens, the answer to that question can be supplied by anyone who has read an essay on Tennyson's poems written in 1855 by George Brimley, the Librarian of Trinity College, Cambridge. Brimley was a critic well above the average of his time in learning and in enlightenment. If he fails anywhere, we can reasonably suppose that on that side the great reading public, less enlightened than he, would fail still more conspicuously. Now, Brimley does fail. He criticises *Claribel*, because Tennyson does not linger on her gentle and affectionate nature, on her grace and beauty. He praises the 1842 volume, because it does not contain *Oenone*. (" Grecian nymphs no longer pour out their loves and griefs to their mother earth.") And he makes a general accusation that the poet's material lacks human interest. If Brimley was saying that in this way, then less kindly and less well-educated readers were saying it more strongly and more stupidly. They were pretty certainly gloating over *Dora* and *The Gardener's Daughter* and turning aside from *Oenone* and the *Lotus Eaters*, and the parts of *In Memoriam* which most certainly conciliated them to Tennyson were the parts which proved that he really was an Englishman who had forgotten Mount Ida for the sake of the Lincolnshire wolds.

It was this sort of interpretation that we to-day must give to those articles in which the critics of the Fifties declared their readiness to welcome new great poets. If the *Edinburgh* said " the English public were never more eager to hail the productions of a literary genius," we must not forget that the *Spectator* had written, " the poet who would really fix the public attention must leave the exhausted past and draw his subjects from matters of present import." That quotation indeed appears in Matthew Arnold's preface to the 1853 poems, and that reminds us that Matthew Arnold had withdrawn the 1852 volume of poems from circulation before fifty copies had been sold, although it contained nearly all of his greatest poetry. The same sort of fate had attended the 1849 volume. This catastrophe could not but rouse our deepest apprehensions on Browning's behalf. The fact is, that the age said that it wished to get itself interpreted—and let it be known that only favourable interpretations would be accepted. If the business, the thoughts, the manner of every-day life were to be handled by the poet, it would be on condition that he avoided " the slightest jar of vulgarity and laughableness." New writers were expected to respect the Established Church at the risk of being thought and called irreverent. No more *Ingoldsby Legends*. And if any poet or critic should turn his attention to the paintings of the old masters, he must not on any account forget—as Ruskin had been guilty of forgetting—that " they were compelled occasionally to address themselves to superstition at the expense of taste." Of Ruskin's famous pamphlet on the Royal Academy Exhibition of 1855 the *Quarterly* reviewer wrote that nothing could be more degradingly low.

Yet again, while great writers were praised on wrong grounds, equally they were blamed on wrong grounds. Dickens himself drew murmurs from his audience because he was perverting the minds of youth by presenting British institutions to them in an unfavourable light. The *Quarterly*, indeed, went so far as to describe him as a Pre-Raphaelite among novelists ; and though that may have been written in praise, it was undoubtedly accepted as a condemnation. Consider again the reception of *Maud*. It looked for a moment as though Tennyson had jeopardised his position. Had he not ascribed to the hero of the poem a passion that is " now and then the passion of a Southern woman rather than an English man ? Would an English man in earnest talk thus ? " Other critics spoke of the " diseased subjectivity " of the poem, and the *Irish Quarterly* said that the poet had approached the bounds which separate reason from idiocy. While some were in this way offended by the content of the poem, others had their teeth set on edge by the form of the verse and could not be reconciled to such lines as—

Now to the scream of a maddened beach dragged down by the
  wave.

Let us further recall how Elizabeth Barrett Browning, whom some thought a likely candidate for the Laureateship, scandalised all respectable women when she published *Aurora Leigh*. They called it a most improper book which no self-respecting person would leave about in the drawing-room.

One might, then, draw out a kind of *Ars Poetica* of

the Fifties. First, to consider the content of poetry the poet must not on any account fail to exhibit in his works a high degree of moral soundness, so that not only those who held to the true doctrine might be edified, but the ignorant and the sceptical might be turned towards the light. The darker side of life might be treated of, but always with a view to the working of some improvement in the social order. Thus Tennyson was justified in describing insanity in *Maud* only because that helped to draw attention to the fact that the lunatic asylums were full. And, as has already been remarked, there must be no attack upon characteristic British institutions.

Originality was a recognised attribute of great art, but mere novelty must be distinguished from true and legitimate originality. Thus it was the craze for novelty which alone could be held to account for the popularity of Ruskin with a certain section of the public. Finally, the slightest suspicion of anything like vulgarity, not to say ribaldry, would suffice to condemn without appeal.

As to the form of poetry, lucidity was one of the first requisites. And, indeed, said the critics, there *was* a curious belief abroad that a poem could not be profound unless it was obscure. Here was the blemish in *In Memoriam* ; and that some reviewers found *Maud* incomprehensible we have already seen. Next to lucidity came finish. There must be unity and coherence in a poem as in all kinds of intellectual products. Even so accomplished a scholar and so conscientious a workman as Matthew Arnold was found on occasion slovenly in his versification. The noblest art was that which subjected itself to the severest discipline. And in this kind the standards had been defined and acknowledged.

Further than this it is not necessary to go. Enough has been said to show us what kind of a reception the Victorian Robert Browning might expect from his Victorian readers. Let us now take up one by one the points in this *Ars Poetica* and consider whether there is any single one upon which he would not be arraigned. The poet must preach sound morals—and here is Browning in the *Statue and the Bust* maintaining that adultery may be laudable ! The *Christian Remembrancer* found much to condemn in him on this side. Did he not, in *Fra Lippo Lippi*, call upon his readers to sympathise with " that licentious monk artist . . . apologising with unctuous minuteness for his shameless course of life." And in general, says the same review, " his pictures of love are coarse passion ; his idea of beauty is sensual." The *Quarterly*, in an article otherwise distinguished by good sense, showed some diffidence in advancing the opinion that in the *Grammarian's Funeral* there was something grand and solemn.

And then Browning had chosen such odd and out-of-the-way subjects—the licentious monk, Fra Lippo Lippi ; the bigot of the *Heretic's Tragedy* ; the shameless prelate in *Saint Praxed's* (a poem which for sheer disgustingness could hardly be equalled), and obscure musicians, Baldassare Galuppi and Master Hugues, of Saxe-Gotha. Evidently Mr. Browning had little sympathy with the Anglican Church : Romanism was much more to his taste. Where, as in *Christmas Eve*, he concerned himself with the central mysteries of Christianity, the language was doggerel and the mood verged upon ribaldry. A sad lack of reverence in Mr. Browning. The *Athenæum*, which did not wholly condemn the poem and found in it a serious vein, likened it to a cathedral " where,

ever as we become absorbed in the anthem the doors
are thrust open to jar us with the common traffic
of the street." That same Hudibrastic versification,
the symbol of a calculated impertinence, defiled
Men and Women no less than the earlier volume.

And what of his treatment of British history and
of British scenery ? There was very little of either
in these volumes. But *Cavalier Lyrics* were pronounced by one reviewer to be mere blackguardry.
Why must the poet harp upon the failings of the
cavaliers and roundheads and not be content to dwell
upon such nobleness as they might have exhibited ?
And why could he not, like Tennyson, make his own
country the background of his poems ? Why not
write poems like *Dora* or *The Gardener's Daughter* ?
Why must it be *Pippa Passes* rather than *Polly Passes* ?
asked the *Quarterly*. In this connection *Fraser's
Magazine* has a passage which deserves to be quoted
in full : " There are fine ballads in the second
volume, healthy and English, clear of that Italianesque pedantry, that *crambe repetita* of olives and
lizards, artists and monks, with which the English
public, for its sins, has been spoon-fed for the last
half-century, ever since Childe Harold in a luckless
hour thought a warmer climate might make him a
better man, and that the way to raise one's own spirit
was to escape to a country where humanity has sunk
below the beasts." Another critic speaks with a
little more caution, but his words are scarcely less
wounding : " The mode of thought, without being
anti-English, constantly bears an indescribable
savour of the Continent."

What the critics had to say about obscurity is
hardly worth repeating. Two points may, indeed,
be noticed. Fraser's reviewer found a word to say

in praise of *Sordello*—not condoning its obscurity, but lamenting that obscurity should have spoilt a noble conception. This was at a time when *Sordello* had been withdrawn by its author from the 1849 volume. Secondly, the poet's obscurity aroused something like real anger. For, that a poet could be at once obscure and a poet was impossible. Browning must be aware of that. If he was not aware of that, it was not for want of admonitions. Yet he persisted in being obscure. It was monstrous—really, Mr. Browning was too proud for anything. For it was not as if the things he had to say could not be said plainly. There was only one possible explanation : he hoped by being obscure to gain a reputation for profundity, just as by being eccentric he would persuade his readers that he was being original.

Likewise the faultiness of his versification proceeded from nothing less than sinful pride. He was too proud to use the crucible and the file, although it was obvious to any intelligent and educated man that the noblest art had always submitted itself willingly to the severest discipline. There was an utter absence in his verse of graceful grammatic flow. And the thought was confused and feeble : " It may seem odd to compare a man so reticent and clever with the weak and loquacious Mrs. Nickleby, but really his random style of address is not unlike that lady's." Random thoughts may sometimes perhaps please if they are expressed in melodious lines—example, " Where Claribel low lieth." But here was nonsense conveyed in harsh cacophonous lines which hardly submitted to be scanned.

The limitation of these reviews are obvious. But

they have not been exhibited here in order to show how low criticism had fallen in the period between *Biographia Litteraria* and *Essays in Criticism*. The object is to illustrate the preconceptions and prejudices which had to be overcome by the more intelligent of the public before they could place themselves in contact with a poet in his poetry. To overcome them was difficult enough in the case of Tennyson or Matthew Arnold ; it was far more difficult in the case of Browning. And in order that the situation may be more fully illustrated from this standpoint, it is well to call to mind not only the grounds upon which Browning was being unintelligently blamed, but also the grounds upon which he was being unintelligently praised.

A ridiculous passage from *Fraser's Review* has already been quoted in which certain poems in the 1849 volume had been approved as " fine ballads, healthy and English " and " free from Italianesque pedantry." The same article, while made uneasy by the morbid atmosphere of *Porphyria's Lover*, considers that the poem is in some measure redeemed by its uncommon pathos. The grounds upon which the *Christian Remembrancer* praised *Any Wife to any Husband* were that, " read with the idea that they represent . . . the greater chance that widows abide in their loneliness than widowers," the poem becomes " not only clear but very beautiful and pathetic." The general tone of that article, in contrast to the savage onslaught delivered in a previous year in the same review, is mildly favourable, and finds in Browning " a votary of mysticism." This description appears to have been fairly common and meant no more than that the language and thought of Browning were hard to grasp, and that the only sure way of grasping them was to assume that when the poet said one thing he meant something quite different. Thus *Any Wife to Any Husband* would never yield up its secret if the readers started with the assumption that the title had any reference to the subject-matter of the poem.. As soon, however, as it was perceived that *Any Wife to Any Husband* really meant *The Chance of Widowers Abiding in their Loneliness*, then the whole significance of the poem leapt out full and clear, and was seen to be very beautiful and pathetic.

But, as might have been expected, it was *Christmas Eve* and *Easter Day* which most surely derailed his critics. *Christmas Eve* was an argument, said one reviewer, for the divinity of Christ ; while another interpreted the same poem as a recommendation to humility and faith. *Fraser's Magazine* contains what is probably the most curious critical document on this subject. The writer confesses that on first reading the poems he had been disappointed. Mr. Browning was known to possess great poetic ability marred by defects which the critics had not failed to point out to him. Surely he would now mend his ways ? Not a bit of it ! Here were " the old levity and irreverence ; the old coarse ungrateful quaint- ness . . . the old obscurity . . . all the old faults, in short, showing more ugly than ever beside the greater sublimity and the intrinsic sweetness with which they have chosen to meddle." And yet at the end of the article come these words : " Thus, step by step, we have passed on from dislike to palliation, from palliation to something like justification." What were these steps from dislike to palliation, from palliation to justification ? There were, in fact, two steps. The first was taken when the critic remem-

bered that at a first reading of *The Princess* he had
been stirred to something like anger; and subsequent readings had convinced him that he was
wrong and that *The Princess* was a fine performance.
Then, having remembered how narrow a shave he
had had with *The Princess*, the writer next remembers
that he is a Christian, and that these poems of
Browning are concerned with the profoundest issues
of religion. There follows this passage. Speaking
of Browning's love for the Christian faith, he says:

" Is it for the critic in such a case to judge harshly
or in love? Must he not say to his own heart, ' Wilt
thou not love one who loves Him, whom thou
professest to love? Take the message as coming NOT
from the poet but from the poet's Lord; and
learn rather than judge: perhaps then thou wilt
find reason to be more contented with the manner
of the message; to believe that thus, and not
otherwise, it was projected upon the mirror of his
brain, because thus, and no otherwise, he could
have uttered it, thrown into it all his peculiar talents,
all the force of his peculiar personality. . . . May
not these very defects be signs of a higher calling
than that of the glib-tongued multitude, whose
rivulets can run smoothly because their channels
are ready scooped and polished for them? Which
is better, he who polishes a doll or he who rough-
hews a colossus? ' "

Concerning the tone of this pronouncement it is
only necessary to say that these are not the words
of a wilfully dishonest man or of a man according
to his own lights uncharitable, but they are a curious
comment upon the blindness of his intelligence.
Not only must he have been unaware of the real
quality of the tone of this paragraph, but he did not

even see that to write it was to abnegate his office of critic. But Nemesis overtook him, for when it came, at the end of his article, to summing up the case and pronouncing a verdict, he can only say that he " remains in doubt what verdict to give, and somewhat glad that our verdict matters so little that it is not worth while giving."

By way of contrast and perhaps for the sake of being just to the men of that age we may turn from these obscure reviewers (but perhaps not the less representative for being obscure) to an intellect of the first order. Carlyle was a warm admirer of Browning—" one of the bravest and most gifted English souls now living " . . . " the finest poetic genius, finest possibility of such, we have got vouchsafed to us in this generation." On 25th April, 1856, Carlyle wrote to Browning acknowledging the present of *Men and Women*.

" My approval was hearty and spontaneous. . . . I shall look far, I believe, to find such a pair of eyes as I see there busy inspecting human life this long while—fresh, valiant, manful character, equipped with rugged humour, just love, just contempt, well carried and bestowed."

He goes on to speak of a genius worth cultivating, " worth sacrificing oneself to tame and subdue into perfection." And this brings him to " the shadow-side of the picture. My friend, it is what they call unintelligibility. That is a fact : you are dreadfully difficult to understand ; and that is really a sin. Admit the fact." Then comes something which may astonish : " I do not at this point any longer forbid you *verse* as I probably once did." He ends up—and these words were written not so very long

before Browning began to think out *The Ring and
the Book*—" If you took up some one *great* subject,
and tasked all your powers upon it for a long while,
vowing to Heaven that you would be plain to the
meanest capacity, then—— ! "

Concerning Dante Gabriel Rossetti's opinions it
will be more convenient to speak in the next chapter.
There remain to be mentioned two other critics who
stand apart from the crowd. Matthew Arnold had
not published any criticism of his contemporary, but
there is matter in his 1853 preface which could have
been quoted both by the enemies of Browning and by
his friends. In favour of Browning is a passage in
which he insists with all his strength that it is no
part of the business of poets to " inflate themselves
with a belief in the pre-eminent greatness and importance of their own times. They do not talk of
their mission, nor of interpreting their age, nor of
the coming poet ; all this, they know, is the mere
delirium of vanity." On the other hand, the poet
must select an excellent action and must achieve the
" clearness of arrangement, rigour of development,
simplicity of style " of the ancients. And on the
whole there is little evidence that Arnold then or
later returned the admiration which Browning
lavished upon him, though it was in accordance
with Browning's recommendation that he restored to
the *New Poems* (in 1867) *Empedocles on Etna*, whose
previous exclusion had provided the theme for the
1853 preface.[1]

The second name is Ruskin, who in the fourth
volume of *Modern Painters* said : " Robert Browning

[1] It may be ominous that Arnold says of Mrs. Browning : " I regard
her as hopelessly confirmed in her aberration from health, nature, beauty
and truth."

is unerring in every sentence he writes about the Middle Ages, always vital, right and profound. . . . I know no other piece of modern English prose or poetry in which there is so much told, as in these lines, of the Renaissance spirit "—nor was it in serious dispraise that he spoke of " those seemingly careless and too rugged lines of his." [1]

When we come to summing up, we find that Browning's admirers in the Fifties were few, but that for the most part they included the greatest minds of his day and the keenest in literary insight. The great mass of people knew nothing of him : the public which read the reviews read in them nothing but condemnation of him ; and one of the severest criticisms passed on him was that he did not appreciate the true worth of his own people and his own age. This ought always to be borne in mind by those—and they are not a few—who call Browning a typical Victorian. For if he was a Victorian, then we may say that he came to his own and his own received him not. But then it may be asked whether indeed he was a Victorian. The answer must be that, in the main, he was. We see now what so many of the Victorians of the Fifties did not see, that although he preferred Pippa to Polly, Tuscany and Fra Lippo Lippi to Surrey and Maclise, olives and Chianti to cheese and beer, yet underneath these superficial matters he had in him much that was characteristic of his age. For in spite of *The Statue and the Bust*, he most firmly and ardently believed in marriage as the true consummation of romantic love, and his moral code was the moral code of the Victorians in its essentials—interpreted, indeed, more intelligently and charitably than by most of the

[1] Browning's reply to Ruskin is discussed in Chapter IV, see pages 132, 133.

3 *11601*

Victorians. He believed in the active life, he
believed in progress and he was ardently patriotic.
He did not like Bohemianism—he hated the circle
of George Sand—and it is probably the *bon bourgeois*
in him that in the end alienated Dante Gabriel
Rossetti from him. For such reasons the general
agreement among critics of to-day in pronouncing
him a representative Victorian is on the whole correct ; or rather it is true of Browning in certain
aspects. In other aspects, to which attention will be
drawn in subsequent chapters, he was not a Victorian. But these aspects, like the Victorian aspect,
passed almost wholly unnoticed by his critics in the
Eighteen-fifties.

CHAPTER III

THE NINETIES

IN 1894 Max Beerbohm cried, " the Victorian era comes to an end." Not that anything final or decisive seems to have happened in that year, but the Nineties did tend to believe that one order of things had passed away and another had taken its place. It is certain that the Eighties had taken a heavy toll of the greater Victorians—Browning, Carlyle, Disraeli, George Eliot and Matthew Arnold ; and Tennyson died in 1892. It is very much less certain that anything which could properly be called a new order had taken their place. Whatever came next after the Victorian era may turn out not to have been an order at all, and certainly it was not new in 1894.

Matthew Arnold had described the early Fifties as a time of spiritual discomfort and an age of bewildering confusion. But if breezes were then disturbing the peace of the garden, they had in the Nineties swollen to the dimensions of a typhoon. To preserve the metaphor, it was *The Origin of Species* which first set the trees rocking violently. How the tempest unchained by these speculations swept with gathering force across the whole domain of thought has often enough been described. There was not in religion, in moral theory, in art, in politics, one single monumental opinion that could seem beyond doubt secure against these blasts. What, for instance, must now be held of man's place in the universe ? Was it any longer certain that he was the sum and crown of things ? Was mind itself, perhaps, no more than a by-product—almost an accident ? Evolutionary methods in general and scientific materialism in particular seemed to be cutting at the very bases of morals because the development of all things high and complex was now being traced from things rudimentary and ignoble, and because that very development was being represented as the work, not of a soul aspiring towards an ideal, but of external non-spiritual forces whose operations might eventually be reducible to a series of mathematical formulæ.

Such a picture of spiritual turmoil is very generally accepted as being true of the decade of the Nineties. But it must not too easily be accepted. The restlessness and the doubt were very roughly speaking in proportion to the intelligence and knowledge of those who felt them. The great majority of the upper middle class, that is to say, the class whose money kept authors and reviewers alive, were not in any great or grave doubt either about the right way of living this life or the right way of assessing poetry. They knew that the beliefs they held most sacred were being assailed, and they did feel some need of being strengthened. They felt like an innocent man conscious of his innocence, but needing a trained barrister—not to assure him of his innocence but to make it clear to others. Besides, there is one curious feature in the general situation which has on the whole tended to escape notice—and that is the kind of attitude which scientists at that time were taking up towards problems of social and individual conduct.

Science at this time was, in a certain sense, in a

condition of stagnation. The main laws governing the physical constitution of the universe were thought to have been discovered. What remained to be done was a huge enough task, but it would in truth be no more than the application of these formulated main laws to phase after phase of existence. And again, though by methods copied from biology, the evolution of institutions, moral codes, religious beliefs was being traced to muddy beginnings, though in that process the authority of religious and ethical systems had been undermined, and was thought by many to be tottering to a crash, yet the main scheme of motives likely to govern the conduct of individuals and communities was not gravely in doubt. The same hands which in the name of truth were overturning the old idols were ready to set them up again in the interests of bio-logical—or sociological—continuity, so that it was hardly in contemplation that praise and blame would be very differently apportioned to this or that act or disposition or that a new hierarchy of virtues would be established. It is true that some few—a very few—were reading Ibsen and Tolstoy, and that even fewer had become aware of the existence of Nietzsche, and that Freud himself was lecturing in the Nineties. If an Englishman of the Nineties—a decent, respect-able doctor or clergyman or schoolmaster—had been asked to name the most redoubtable rebel of the time, he would unhesitatingly have named Huxley. But Huxley's influence, outside the region of science proper, was wholly negative : in some ways it was not even negative. In the matter of a code of morals, or more generally in respect of the art of living, Huxley had nothing to offer which could reasonably be judged contrary to the precepts of the Established Church.

It is in this broad setting that the poetical thought of the Nineties must be placed. And in order to do that the more conveniently, it may be well to distinguish between two classes of opinions or attitudes —on the one hand, those of the more powerful and advanced minds, of men whose names remain with us because they seem to have opened up new paths ; and, on the other hand, those of the great mass of more or less educated critics and readers of poetry. This, in effect, is what we did in the case of the Eighteen-fifties, but in dealing with the Nineties the available material is so much richer and more complex that a separate chapter seems to be demanded for each class. The present chapter therefore will be confined to discussing the thoughts and the influence of a few men whom we consider characteristic of that age, the chapter next following will deal with that far larger aggregate which can only be described by such a vague phrase as " the intelligent reading public."

In the present chapter, then, an attempt will be made first, to suggest what forces were at work in bringing to birth new ideas of the function and value of poetry, and secondly, to deduce from these ideas a critique of Browning's poetry (in other words to answer the question, " What might men with such ideas be expected to think of Browning ? "), and thirdly, to examine the critical estimates actually formed by the men who had given birth to these ideas (that is, to answer the question, " What, in fact, did these men think of Browning ? ").

The previous chapter spoke of the pride of Mid-Victorians in their material progress. They felt confident that the path in which they had set their feet must lead to prosperity and happiness for the whole community. Much had to be done, and there

was need of courage and perseverance, but the day
was not far off when ignorance, poverty and vice
would melt away from the face of the land.   And the
Nineties saw that it was not so.   Especially did clear-
eyed and sensitive young men see that it was not so.
The fruits of disillusionment were various.   Some—
who earned the name of the Decadent Æsthetes [1]—
turned their faces away from the ugly realities of life
and tried to create for themselves an artificial
paradise.   Others, disgusted with all that had been
achieved in the name of reason, looked in another
direction for consolation—in a twilight where reason
did not rule and dreams were truer and more life-
giving than the hours of waking.   Any tendency
which men or groups of men exhibit to shut themselves away in their art from the general endeavour
of their kind—to disown any preoccupation with
problems of conduct or religion as such—would be
strongly reinforced by the doctrine of " Art for Art's
sake," which in the Eighties had been proclaimed by
Whistler.   His absurd suit for libel against Ruskin
had delighted a younger generation, who felt sure
than an æsthetic must be profoundly vicious which
condemned Rembrandt for the immorality of his
colouring.   Up, they cried, with Japanese prints and
Velasquez and down with Carpaccio and the guilds of
stone-masons.   The divorce of arts from morals was
pronounced absolute.   This, as we shall see in
Chapter V, where reference is made to the theory of
Poetry for Poetry's sake, led to an overwhelming
insistence on technique.   The subject-matter of

[1] Whether there was ever anything which could properly be called a
Decadent or Decadent Æsthete Movement (in the sense in which there
was a Romantic Movement) is very doubtful.   Yet it is certain that
Wilde and Beardsley had a following, and that there was formed under
such influences a body of ideas not easily to be measured or defined
which for the sake of convenience may be called Decadent Æsthete.

poetry became a thing of little importance : it was
the treatment which counted.

We have now to notice in the Nineties the existence of yet a third group, more robust and practical,
preaching a new kind of realism.   They summoned
their friends to see the world as it was, stripped of
sham ideals, and they called for immediate and
strenuous action for the setting up of a new code.
What is common to these three groups is a belief that
their own generation either was not worth saving or
could only be saved by painful sacrifices and a
purgation of fire.   But not all of the younger writers
despaired of their generation.   One at least, and he
in some ways had the most influence upon the reading public, saw hope in the creation of a great Empire,
and preached a curious mixture of realism and
romanticism, of materialism and spiritualism.   Finally, we discern another group—if they can be called
a group—of thinkers not attaching themselves to any
particular movement, but each going his own way.
The influence of these men did not make itself fully
felt in the Nineties.

It is important to consider each of these groups in
a little detail, and that in the order in which they
have just been named.   The Decadents developed
tendencies which can be traced back through
Swinburne to the Pre-Raphaelites.   From their
inception, these tendencies swerved away from the
main social tendencies of the age.   The Pre-
Raphaelites did not like, they detested, the industrial and commercial prosperity of the Fifties—
the concernment with material ends, the conscious
and self-confident break with the past, the excited
straining towards a future in which aerial navies
would grapple in the blue and all India's teeming

millions would go clad in Manchester cotton goods. From all this they swerved away ; and if they could not anywhere outside them and in the present find things that contented eye and ear, they sought them in other countries and in the past. Hence a certain exoticism in their poetry and that element in it which has not very happily been named mediævalism. The exoticism was special in the sense that these poets did at times surrender themselves more completely to the direct influence of foreign literatures. It was not only that they sought themes from abroad and laid the scenes of their poems in foreign countries, aiming at " local colour." That had often enough been done. It was that in a peculiar degree they tried to fit themselves to the temper of foreign writers and to borrow from them a part of their technique. This tendency, which they did not, indeed, carry very far, was to be continued and developed by Swinburne and carried to its extreme by the Decadents. With Swinburne and the Decadents the prevailing influence was a French influence. In Hugo and in Baudelaire Swinburne discerned attitudes towards which his own nature was spontaneously growing. He was encouraged to attempt a more absolute divorce between poetry and morals than the Pre-Raphaelites had effected, a completer dedication to vividness and intensity of sensation, a more conscientious resolve to leave nothing unexplored within the range of experience, and particularly within the entire range of the passions. Consequently he shocked the British public. It is not easy for us to imagine, at a distance of two generations, the veiled horror and the shrieks of protest with which the 1866 volume of *Poems and Ballads* was greeted by a public, many of whom were still doubtful about the moral soundness of *The Statue and the Bust*, and only with an effort could stomach the " diseased subjectivity " of *Maud*.

The Decadents may be looked upon as the spiritual heirs of Swinburne. They went a step farther than he, and courted a catastrophe. Their influence tends, perhaps, to be a little underrated at this day. Certainly it cannot be said that they left no trace of themselves upon the texture of the general thought. That it is still easy to laugh at them is proved by the continued popularity of *Patience*, but, as we have seen, they stood for something which persists to-day and is the subject of anything but laughter—they stood for disillusionment. It drove them everywhere in search of a new sensation. They discovered emptiness.

" There is no such thing," wrote Oscar Wilde, " as romantic experience. There are romantic memories and there is the desire of romance—that is all. Our most fiery moments of ecstacy are merely shadows of what somewhere else we have felt, or of what we long some day to feel. . . . And strangely enough, what comes of this is a curious mixture of ardour and indifference—I myself would sacrifice everything for a new experience, and I know there is no such thing as a new experience at all."

In the attempt to make for themselves a paradise of new sensations they determined to refuse no means lawful or unlawful—but especially unlawful. For help in their task they betook themselves to Nerval and to Baudelaire. In Théophile Gautier's famous introduction to the *Fleurs du Mal* they found their dogma finally stated. There were also their own spiritual brethren, the Symbolistes-Décadents, and

especially there was Huysmans's *A Rebours*, of which
it is written by Oscar Wilde that " things dimly
dreamed of were suddenly made real in it."

The second group of thinkers also shrank from
surveying the plight into which the world had fallen.
The movement of their thought is quieter and more
dreamy. Trouble has come on the world, because
men have been blind to the forces, more powerful
than reason, which sway the spirit. Ardour and
inspiration must give way to a kind of mystical contemplation, reason must be dethroned in favour of
intuition.

> What of all the will to do ?
>   It has vanished long ago,
> For a dream-shaft pierced it through
>   From the unknown Archer's bow.
>
> What of all the soul to think ?
>   Some one offered it a cup
> Filled with a diviner drink,
>   And the flame has burned it up.
>
> What of all the hope to climb ?
>   Only in the self we grope
> To the misty end of time :
>   Truth has put an end to hope.

So sings A. E., and Yeats has much of the same tone
concerning—

> The dim wisdoms old and deep
> That God gives man in sleep.

And the moment, 1893, was favourable for the
publication of *The Celtic Twilight*. It is interesting
to note that these thinkers have also their affinities
with France. Yeats had become acquainted with
that crazy charlatan who named himself " Sar
Péladan," the Rosicrucian mystic. But Yeats de-

liberately and persistently drew his main inspiration,
not from abroad, but from his native land and folk-
lore. The feature in his thought which most
attracted the attention of his English readers was
certainly a constant preoccupation with a world of
disembodied spirits surrounding man on every side,
a world not ruled by laws that he has learnt to obey,
a world of wonder and terror into which he may at
any moment be rapt away. But the poet might find
in this spirit world, in this dream world, a beauty,
a truth and a freedom that his workaday hours could
not know.

> As thus our songs arose : " You stars
> Across your wandering ruby cars
> Shake the loose reins : you slaves of God,
> He rules you with an iron rod,
> He holds you with an iron bond,
> Each one woven to the other,
> Each one woven to his brother,
> Like bubbles on a frozen pond ;
> But we in a lovely land abide
> Unchainable as the dim tide,
> With hearts that know nor law nor rule
> And hands that hold no wearisome tool,
> Folded in love that knows no morrow,
> Nor the gray wandering osprey sorrow."

And yet again this voice forbids us to hunger fiercely
after truth ; and there is one utterance of Yeats to be
quoted here which will gain a new significance when
we come to consider our own plight in this day :

> Seek then
> No learning from the starry men
> Who follow with the optic glass
> The whirling ways of stars that pass
>
> Dream, dream, for this is also sooth.

It is from this point perhaps that the revival of
mysticism in poetry contemporary with ourselves

can be traced, although in the years between then and
now other influences were certainly at work, besides
the Celtic Twilight of Yeats, A.E. and Fiona Macleod
—for instance, the poetry of Francis Thompson, of
whom it was written that " His only realities were
spiritual ; his only adventures in the land of visions."

But there are other attitudes besides those of
despair or of mystic withdrawal to be distinguished
in the literature of this moment. In 1891 George
Bernard Shaw published *The Quintessence of Ibsenism*
and in the following year *Widowers' Houses*. As the
Decadents had found their affinities in Baudelaire and
the Symbolistes-Décadents, so did Shaw in Ibsen
and in Schopenhauer. But of all the motives of his
mind which so rudely shocked the public of the
Nineties, that which must concern us in this context
is his attack upon romanticism and idealism. " The
idealist," he wrote, " is a more dangerous man than
the Philistine, just as a man is a more dangerous
animal than a sheep." And again, " Our ideals, like
the gods of old, are constantly demanding human
sacrifices." But while he attacks idealism, he rejects
materialism and realism. How the recoil from
these two philosophies had affected his fellow-
countrymen and driven them to the worship of
dreams has already been hinted. But Shaw does
not follow them here. Reason, which he describes
as Dagon, Moloch and Jehovah rolled into one, is
deposed in favour of the will to live. And it is
because materialism leaves no room within its
galvanised iron ash-bin for the " will to live " that
he will have none of it. He is a realist in the sense
that he believes in the importance of seeing things
as they are and of destroying all shams—especially
sham ideals and sham romance. While in *The*

Quintessence of Ibsenism a distinct flavour of Nietzsche
is discernible, Shaw had not even heard of that
philosopher in 1891. This is worth noting because
he himself makes this comment: " I attach great
importance to the evidence that the movement
voiced by Schopenhauer, Wagner, Ibsen, Nietzsche
and Strindberg was a world movement, and would
have found expression if every one of those writers
had perished in his cradle."

But none of the writers hitherto mentioned could
in the Nineties command the same attention from the
general public as Rudyard Kipling. Here is a
curious mixture of realism and romance—a determination to see in life, as it was then developing, a
hope of greatness and beauty. There is, then, in
Kipling, no revolt against the mechanisation of life,
or against preoccupation with material interests,
but a belief that these tendencies can run in harness
with a high idealism. This harmonious co-opera-
tion he found embodied in the British Empire. That
Empire stood for commercial and industrial expan-
sion, but, far more important, it stood for the propa-
gation of a special view of life, for the ideals of
chivalry, with their attendant virtues of endurance
and adventurousness. By one people alone, by the
British, had these ideals been assimilated. As for
others—the lesser tribes without the Law—they
must give way or be crushed. And the list of
virtues of the chosen people included discipline and
the immediate recognition of the greater man by his
weaker brethren. As the Chosen Race must lord it
over the Gentiles, so within the Race the greater
man must rule the weaker. But Kipling did not
deliberately shut his eyes to weaknesses and imperfections. If he believed—as he did passionately

believe—in the British supremacy in India, he saw also virtues in the native races and corruption in the rulers. He sings the glory of adventurous travel, but no one has drawn more faithful pictures of the incidental hardships and degradations. The poet who really believed that the Lord had given the British dominion over palm and pine also painted the portrait of Badalia Herodsfoot.

Finally—to close this brief and precarious review of the new movements or tendencies—we discern two or three figures standing in a sense apart and not forming a group or attracting much comment. There is no good reason why much space should be devoted to them here. The day of Thomas Hardy was not yet ; there will be more to say of him when the Nineteen-twenties are being dealt with. The position of Meredith is one of the puzzles of literary history. Philosophically he belongs to the decade of the Nineties more than any of the great names hitherto mentioned ; for in that aspect he seems to be grouped with Huxley and Herbert Spencer. There were few writers of the time more highly esteemed by the greater of his contemporaries ; there are few who seem to have had less influence on his contemporaries or on the next generation. It is as if by some curious irony of destiny he had succeeded in removing himself further from what was vital and fruitful in the thought of his time than the remotest and mistiest of the Celtic Twilight group. And yet, as we have said, in certain aspects he is more the man of the late Nineteenth Century than Wilde or Henley or Francis Thompson. Except to note that he was a lover of Browning and that Browning admired the originality and force of his earlier poetry, we need not linger with him.

Of Walter Pater rather more falls to be said. It may seem that in a logical arrangement he would have been grouped with the Decadent Æsthetes because there was so much in his thought and in his manner which was bound to have a strong appeal to them—for instance, the careful deliberate reflection upon an inner experience, the remoteness from contemporary political or social issues, and above all the preciousness of style and the refinement of taste in measuring and valuing the minutest differences of sensation and impression. " Experience," he said, " is ringed round for each one of us by that thick wall of personality through which no real voice has ever pierced on its way to us, or from us to that which we can only conjecture to be without. Every one of those impressions is the impression of an individual in his isolation, each mind keeping as a solitary prisoner its own dream of a world." Elsewhere in the same essay, " A counted number of pulses only is given us of a variegated dramatic life. How may we see in them all that is to be seen in them by the finest senses ? How shall we pass most swiftly from point to point and be present always at the focus where the greatest number of vital forces unite in their purest energy ? To burn always with this hard gem-like flame, to maintain this ecstacy, is success in life." Such a doctrine of swift brilliance, at once hard and uneasy, reads like a passage from a Decadent manifesto. Pater was very well aware of this, and that was the reason why he cut out the essay from the second edition of *The Renaissance*. However, the words had been written and cannot be wiped out. They reveal a temper of thought which it is hardly unjust to call artificiality —paradoxical as that may seem in a writer who

so insistently maintained the artist's obligation of
sincerity.

But the chief reason why Pater could not be
omitted from this part of our study is not his affinity
with the Decadents, but the new doctrine of criticism
which he set up and which in our own time may be
said to have established itself irremovably. Criticism
is to become subjective. The new critic does not
ask what is Aristotle's pleasure in the matter. He
will not accept the ruling of Coleridge and apply it
to whatever work he may be considering. He must
look not outwards to a received dogma, but inwards
to his own impressions. He asks, in Pater's own
words, " What is this song or picture, this engaging
personality presented in life or book, to me ? Does
it give me pleasure ? If so, what sort and degree of
pleasure ? How is my nature modified by its
presence and under its influence ? " Professor
Saintsbury has drawn out in all its detail the history
of the development of this critical attitude. If in a
certain sense it was no new thing, yet this way of
expressing it, this full and direct expression of it, was
new for the public who read the essays in *The
Renaissance*.

The attempt has been made to group the new
tendencies of critical thought in this decade, and
according to the plan laid down the time has come to
inquire concerning each group first, what estimate it
might have been expected to form of the poetry of
Browning, and, secondly, what estimate it did
actually form.

It has been suggested that in most of the groups a
strong sense of disillusionment is present. Towards
the end of his life it is clear that Browning himself
felt the temptation to despair. But he overcame it

4

and it would be a freak of criticism to pretend that
his general optimism was ever modified in any important respect.   Nor again could it be hoped that
the Decadents with their ideal of artificiality would
find in him any sort of encouragement.   Browning
also had his paradise, but there was nothing artificial
in it.   And though he desired new experiences, they
were not such as would attract Oscar Wilde.   His
attitude towards new experiences may be brought out
by comparing him in this respect with the Decadents'
patron saint, Baudelaire.   Let us attempt to read,
in the light of Browning's attitude to life, the conclusion of Baudelaire's *La Mort*.   The first stanza
of it might almost have been written by Browning.
It is easy to imagine him saying in his own way :

>   O Mort, vieux capitaine, il est temps ! levons l'ancre.

And again the epilogue to *Fifine* (*The Householder*)
with its cry—

>   Ah, but if you knew how time has dragged, days, nights !
>   .   .   .   .   .   .
>   If you knew but how I dwelt down here !

might be compared with—

>   Ce pays nous ennuie, O Mort !   Appareillons.

And the next two lines can also be read as Browning—

>   Si le ciel et la mer sont noirs comme de l'encre,
>   Nos cœurs que tu connais sont remplis de rayons !

But at the second verse the comparison breaks down,
for the poet who wrote his *Epilogue* to *Asolando* stood
at the very opposite pole of thought from the poet
who wrote :

Verse nous ton poison pour qú' il nous réconforte !
Nous voulons, tant ce feu nous brûle le cerveau,
Plonger au fond du gouffre, Enfer on Ciel, qú' importe ?
Au fond de l'Inconnu pour trouver du *nouveau*.[1]

But this latter mood is the mood of the Decadents. And like Baudelaire they knew that this " new thing " would never be accorded—" there is no such thing as a new experience." But in actual fact the Decadents did not attack, they did not even disown, Browning. In view of what is to follow in later chapters, it is worth while collecting the evidence for this statement. The first point to be noted is that it was, perhaps, in their tradition to read Browning. For their tradition, as we have seen, was handed down to them from the Pre-Raphaelites through Swinburne. Rossetti had admired *Pauline* so much that he transcribed the whole of it in the British Museum ; and he wrote to ask Browning if he was the author. " To him it seemed the work of an unconscious pre-Raphælite," says Professor Herford. " My brother," says W. M. Rossetti, " by readings, recitations and preachments, imposed Browning as a sort of dogmatic standard upon the P.R.B." And William Morris wrote in the poet's praise in the Oxford and Cambridge Magazine.

The case of Swinburne is rather less simple. He began by admiring Browning, and M. Georges Lafourcade has traced influences of Browning's style in some of the earlier poems. Then there is, in 1875, the essay on Chapman, in which he discusses Browning's merits or defects as a dramatic poet. The passage in question begins by rebutting the

---

[1] As a matter of fact, Browning would have approved of anyone who boldly and with all his energies pressed on to any goal he had proposed himself—*The Statue and the Bust* proves this. But he would not have made a sonnet, but a long psychological study.

charge of obscurity so constantly levelled at Browning. One characteristic sentence at least must be
quoted : " He is something too much the reverse
of obscure ; he is too brilliant and subtle for the
ready reader of a ready writer to follow with any
certainty the track of an intelligence which moves
with such incessant rapidity, or even to realise with
what spiderlike swiftness and sagacity his building
spirit leaps and lightens to and fro and backward
and forward as it lives along the animated line of his
labour, springs from thread to thread and darts
from centre to circumference of the glittering and
quivering web of living thought woven from the
inexhaustible stores of his perception and kindled
from the inexhaustible fire of his imagination." But
he is not in the strict sense a dramatist so much as a
practising barrister. He had " an unique and in-
comparable genius of analysis," but he represents his
characters as analysing themselves and expressing the
results of their analysis with an insight and a delicacy
and a thoroughness of which they were incapable.

And in Swinburne's sonnet sequence, written just
after Browning's death, the greatness which he
chiefly praises is this :

> O Spirit of man, what mystery moves in thee
> That he might know not of in spirit, and see
> The heart within the heart that seems to strive. . . .

Oscar Wilde, then, is almost following a tradition
when he praises Browning, and, like Swinburne's,
his praise also is qualified. In an article originally
published in the *Nineteenth Century* he wrote :
" Taken as a whole the man was great . . . he is the
most Shakesperean creature since Shakespeare. If
Shakespeare could sing with a myriad lips, Browning

could stammer through a thousand mouths." When later on this critique was incorporated in *Intentions* and took the form of a dialogue, Wilde added this passage :

> *Ernest* : There is something in what you say, but there is not everything in what you say. In many points you are unjust.
> *Gilbert* : It is difficult not to be unjust to what one loves.[1]

Wilde, too, anticipating the judgment of Henry James twenty years later, prophesies that Browning will be remembered as a writer of fiction. This calls up to his mind another writer also much talked of for his obscurity, George Meredith, and he concludes his paragraph with a characteristic epigram, " Meredith is a prose Browning, and so is Browning." But though he does not in this essay make any special reference to Browning's psychological insight, he says in one of his letters—referring to a previous meeting with his correspondent, " It was an hour intensely dramatic and intensely psychological— and, in art, only Browning can make action and psychology one." And again, " In our meeting there was a touch of Browning—keen curiosity, wonder, delight."

The main qualification which Wilde makes in his praise of Browning is that his technique falls so far short of perfection and that on this account he will not be remembered as a poet. His chief praise is for the variety and scope of his work. " Taken as a whole, the man was great . . ." What surprises in this criticism is that the admirer of Huysmans should not have dwelt upon certain features in Browning's

---

[1] Is it mere fancy to connect this with these lines from Browning's lyrical epilogue to *The Melon Seller* (*Ferishtah's Fancies*) ?

> Be unjust for once, Love ! Bear it—and I may
> . . . .
> Oh, so all unjust,—the less deserved, the more divine.

work which in spirit and intuition come so close to
the work of the French author. There is, for one
thing, Browning's joy in rich textures and in gorgeous
colours. A score of passages could be quoted in
illustration of this—for example :

> Who has not heard how Tyrian shells
>   Enclosed the blue, that dye of dyes
> Whereof one drop worked miracles,
>   And coloured like Astarte's eyes
> Raw silk the merchant sells ?
>
>   .   .   .   .
>
> Enough to furnish Solomon
>   Such hangings for his cedar house,
> That when gold-robed he took the throne
>   In that abyss of blue, the Spouse
> Might swear his presence shone
>
> Most like the centre-spike of gold
>   Which burns deep in the bluebell's womb,
> What time, with ardours manifold
>   The bee goes singing to her groom,
> Drunken and overbold.

How comes it that Wilde overlooked *Childe Roland*,
where phrase after phrase reminds one of Huysmans's
love of " les sites lépreux ? "

> As for the grass, it grew as scant as hair
>   In leprosy ; thin dry blades pricked the mud,
>   Which underneath looked kneaded up with blood.
> One stiff blind horse, his every bone a-stare,
> Stood stupefied, however he came there :
>   Thrust out past service from the devil's stud !

Could the lover of Baudelaire have avoided mentioning another surprising parallel? In *Amphibian*
comes this :

> What if a certain soul
>   Which early slipped its sheath,
> And has for its home the whole
>   Of heaven, thus look beneath,

> Thus watch one who in the world,
>   Both lives and likes life's way
>   .   .   .   .
> But sometimes when the weather
>   Is blue and warm waves tempt
> To free oneself of tether
>   And try a life exempt
>
> From worldly noise and dust,
>   In the sphere which overbrims
> With passion and thought,—why, just
>   Unable to fly, one swims !

And in *Spleen et Idéal* (III *Elévation*) Baudelaire writes :

> Au dessus des étangs, au dessus des vallées
> Des montagnes, des bois, des nuages, des mers . . .
> .   .   .   .
> Mon esprit, tu te meus avec agilité,
> Et comme un bon nageur qui se pâme dans l'onde,
> Tu sillonnes gaîment l'immensité profonde. . . .

And the horse in *Childe Roland* is worthy to be set side by side with the horse in Baudelaire's *Une Gravure Fantastique*.

> Sans éperons, sans fouet, il essouffle un cheval
> Fantôme comme lui, rosse apocalyptique,
> Qui bave des naseaux comme un épileptique.

It is certain that when these lines are restored to their context, the total effect is in the two poets hopelessly irreconcilable, but they indicate some sort of common ground in particulars of the imagination. One might have expected the Decadents to note such things in Browning, if only to lament that they were allied to a point of view in their eyes so false and worthless. The probable explanation seems to be that Oscar Wilde and those who saw life as he saw it were blind to such qualities in Browning because they had not gone to look for them. Probably they did not trouble very much to question the accepted view of Browning as a champion of conventional morality, an optimist, a stranger even if a distinguished stranger.

Among other contributors to the *Yellow Book* was Arthur Symons, whose book on Symbolism shows his strong sympathies with the literature of those French poets whose work was exercising a strong influence on the Decadent Æsthetes. Yet in his book, *An Introduction to the Study of Browning*, there is nothing to make any reader suspect that he was not in complete sympathy with the general attitude and the critical standards of the Browning Society itself. Actually this book was written in 1886, but as in the preface to the second edition, in 1906, the author says that his views on Browning as a poet have not changed, we may be justified in mentioning it in this chapter. Like Wilde, he compares Browning with Shakespeare—but without Wilde's qualifications. He notes the unity of conception of all the vast mass of his work, explains the special dramatic quality of it, notes the keenness of his perception of motive, the range and variety of his poetry, and defends him at length against the accusations of obscurity and lack of artistry. It is hardly an exaggeration to say that, judging his poet as a whole, he will admit of no imperfections in him.

Of the " Celtics," William Sharp had been a personal friend of Browning. He wrote a monograph, and a memorial poem, but both of these in the days before Fiona Macleod had come into being. There is not easily distinguishable, either in the monograph or in the memorial poem, any characteristic " Celtic " tendency of thought or emotion.

And, indeed, from the rest of this group of writers
came no definite and direct expression of opinion
on Browning. On the other hand, Francis Thompson praised him in an article in the *Academy*.
After Wilde's epigram about the prose Browning,
Thompson's verdict falls wholly flat—that Browning
is a verse Meredith. He names Browning " an indis-
putable poet," and denies that he " had or thought
himself to have any message " for his public. And
in a certain sense this denial of a message is true and
salutary. It is true as regards any work of Browning's which is genuinely dramatic : and in this
regard it is salutary because of the almost universal
tendency in those times to quote as Browning's views
the views of any and all of the characters he brought
on to his stage. But in the concluding part of *The
Ring and the Book* Browning in his own person de-
livers a message to the public which liked him not.
And the message sounds curiously discrepant from
what was in those days—and has been since those
days—the accepted notion of Browning's teaching.

> So British public, who may like me yet,
> (Marry and amen !) learn one lesson hence
> Of many which whatever lives should teach :
> This lesson, that our human speech is naught,
> Our human testimony false, our fame
> And human estimation words and wind.

And the whole of *La Saisiaz* is a message—a
message of hope. That he might make it more
effectual, Browning longs for fame :

Fame ! Then give me fame, a moment ! As I gather at a glance
Human glory after glory vivifying yon expanse,
Let me grasp them all together, hold on high and brandish well
Beacon-like above the rapt world ready, whether heaven or hell
Send the blazing summons earthwards, to submit itself the same.

How to explain Thompson's blindness to all this ?
Only by supposing that he, like Oscar Wilde, brought
preconceived notions to his survey of Browning.
Wilde's preconceived notions came from outside
himself—from the general opinion. Thompson's
came from within himself, from his meditations
upon what poetry should not be, namely a sermon in
verse.

George Bernard Shaw was a member of the
Browning Society. It is true that he was a disruptive
element, but he did desire that his fellow-members
should " read their Browning." Judging by the
evidence of the " Papers," he hardly ever spoke at a
meeting without shocking the Society. He shocked
them by declaring that Browning was not a great
dramatic poet. In proof he cited *Caliban upon
Setebos*. Caliban, he said, as depicted by Browning,
combined " the introspective powers of a Hamlet "
with the " theology of an evangelical Churchman."
Now, it was unthinkable that an evangelical Churchman should have the introspective powers of a
Hamlet. There is a resemblance here to the view
expressed by Swinburne in the Chapman essay. In
Caliban upon Setebos Browning is in effect pleading
Caliban's cause, as a barrister might plead it ; he
could see into the machinery of that savage mind
and expose its workings with a completeness and
certainty of which the savage himself would have
been incapable. Perhaps it was this keenness of
vision which attracted Shaw, and the fact that
Browning was no dreamer in the ordinary sense of
that word. It may be—there cannot be certainty on
the point—that Browning's own view concerning
poets and dreamers is uttered by Don Juan in
Fifine at the Fair.

> A poet never dreams :
> We prose folk always do : we miss the proper duct
> For thoughts on things unseen . . .
> . . . What ghosts do poets see ?
> What daemons fear ?   What man or thing misapprehend ?

But his wide-awake eyes certainly did not see what to the eyes of George Bernard Shaw was so clear : they did not see through romance to the Life Force. He was not a realist—nor is Shaw : he did not exalt reason above other faculties (Dean Inge calls him a misologist)—and what Shaw said about reason has already been quoted.

That Rudyard Kipling felt the influence of Browning can be proved from his own poems ; and one recalls the delight with which Beetle discovered *Men and Women* in the Head's library. We are not told whether Beetle (who is said to be a projection of some part of his creator's personality) was affected by *La Saisiaz*. One of Kipling's greatest stories *At the End of the Passage* closes with a quotation from *Cristina*. After the dreadful episode of Hummil dying in an agonised and terrifying dream, as his three friends are preparing to ride away to their several stations, one of them, Spurstow, sums up the situation thus :

> There may be Heaven : there must be Hell :
> Meanwhile we have our life here.   We-ell ?

This is a curious instance of misquotation. The words are exact, but the punctuation is wrong. For the mark of interrogation replaces an exclamation mark in the original poem. What Spurstow meant by " We-ell ? " is—" Is there anything to add ? " or " What shall we do about it ? " or some such question. What Browning meant by " Well ! " is

" So be it. It is well ! "   And that exclamation
would not have been at all appropriate at the end of
Kipling's story.   But from Browning, the poet of
imperialism gained, and could have gained, little
beyond delight in the poems for themselves, for their
vitality, their colour, their technique and especially
their vocabulary.   Browning—unless we make a
doubtful exception of a few of the earlier poems—
might never have heard of the British Empire, and
there is no evidence that he believed that the
happiness of the world depended upon the British
code of conduct being imposed upon all other
peoples.

As for Walter Pater, there seems little enough in
common between him and the fighting poet.   Nevertheless, Pater had spoken strong words of praise in
his essay on Winckelmann in *The Renaissance*.   It
is the artistry of Browning which he there praises.
" The base of all artistic genius," he says, " is the
power . . . of putting a happy world of its own
creation in place of the meaner world of common
days."   This function poetry can accomplish " in
the choice and development of some special situation
which lifts or glorifies a character, in itself poetical.
. . . The poems of Robert Browning supply
brilliant examples of this power.   His poetry is pre-
eminently the poetry of situations."   It is in the
character of Pater to see in Browning the special
power of substituting for the grey and tasteless
realities of life a poetical world more highly coloured
and of a fuller savour.   He praises *Le Byron de nos
Jours* because in it " an artificial light is constructed
and broken over the chosen situation. . . ."   This
was in 1873.   Thirteen years later he reviewed in
the *Guardian* Arthur Symons's *Introduction to the*

Study of Browning. And any attentive reader of Marius the Epicurean would find it hard not to gasp in his surprise when, turning to this *Guardian* essay, he found the following sentence—" Certainly, we shall not quarrel with Mr. Symons for reckoning Mr. Browning, among English poets, second to Shakespeare alone. . . ." What immediately follows in the text might possibly be stretched to mean that Pater was thinking of the quantity rather than the quality of Browning's work. Nevertheless, his praise is genuine and makes no reserves. " Mr. Symons," he says, " is right in laying emphasis on the grace, the finished skill, the music, native and ever ready to the poet himself—tender, manly, humorous, awe-stricken—when speaking in his own proper person." The highest praise he bestows on *Pippa Passes* and *Men and Women*. But, to revert, such a verdict as this is a little surprising from the Neo-Cyrenaic, from the critic who is held by some to have erred in attempting to approximate the function of poetry too closely to the function of music. That he did not regard Browning's melody as impeccable might be thought likely on general grounds, and also from the fact that in speaking of the interest in music shown in *Master Hugues of Saxe-Gotha*, *Abt Vogler* and so on, he is careful to say that it is Browning's interest in music which is unique. And yet there is no ambiguity in the phrase " the music, native and ever ready to the poet himself." The curious contrast—noted by another critic (anonymous) of this time—between Browning's love and intimate knowledge of music and his rough unmelodious verse would surely, if it had been present to his consciousness, have been noted by the man who said that " all art constantly aspires towards the condition of music ; music being the typical or ideally consummate art."

To sum up, the contributions made to Browning criticism by the leading minds of this decade are not remarkable for originality, nor do they seem likely to be of permanent value. That these men should have had comparatively little to say of Browning is peculiar. It is peculiar because there was so much in the poet which might have been expected to draw their fiercest attacks, and there were some things which might have been expected to win their admiration. Wilde and those who followed him did not attack the optimism of Browning nor the bourgeois element in much of his work. How eloquent might they have grown over the fact that one of Browning's favourite novels was *Madame Bovary* ! They do not even seem to have known that. Then there were certain poems which, by a slight and almost pardonable distortion, they could have represented as prophecies of their own kingdom of the artificial. Yet again we have seen the curious inconsistencies of Pater in his *Guardian* article ; and to that we may add this remark that the critic did not appear to realise how closely in spirit he was walking with the poet in making it a cardinal doctrine of his criticism that for each of us experience is ringed round by a wall of personality. He had forgotten—

What though fancy scarce may grapple with the complex and immense
" His own world for every mortal " ?

and again—

Knowledge stands on my experience : all outside its narrow hem,
Free surmise may sport and welcome . . .

We seem to find repeated in this decade the anomaly which we remarked in the critical background of the Fifties—that is to say, the failure to apply its own characteristic critical standards to the poet's work. In both decades what surprises us is that this element which ought to have been pronounced a defect (one would think) and that other which might have been praised go unnoticed or are differently interpreted. Perhaps we shall find the same anomaly when we come to examine the attitude of less distinguished readers of the poet.

CHAPTER IV

THE NINETIES (*Continued*)

THE BROWNING SOCIETY—J. T. NETTLE-SHIP—MRS. ORR

M. GEORGES LAFOURCADE reproduces in *La Jeunesse de Swinburne* the following fragment which has been preserved in Mr. T. J. Wise's collection :

> Thus runs our wise men's song :
> Being dark, it must be light
> And most things are so wrong
> That all things must be right ;
> God must mean well, he works so ill by this world's laws.
>
> This, when our souls are drowning,
> Falls on them like a benison ;
> This satisfies our Browning
> And this delights our Tennyson :
> And soothed Britannia simpers in serene applause.

And certainly, if there was any truth in the opening passage of the last chapter, Britannia had need of soothing. She felt there were in her midst anarchists who threatened her with the dissolution of all that had seemed most stable and necessary in her thought. In this time of distress she rallied her champions ; and in that band she counted Tennyson and Browning. Their greatness as poets had been firmly established, and they had even been by some ranked with Shakespeare and Milton. The tendency, which had prevailed through so many centuries, to believe that a great poet is a great teacher, was strengthened in an age in which a majority of the reading public felt the need of being reassured and strengthened in matters of religion and morality. They wanted to be reassured that man was immortal, that there was a God, that the old moral ideals were not illusive, that the established hierarchy of virtues had not been upset—in short, that God was in His Heaven and all was right with the world. If in this frame of mind they read the two poets, it was almost inevitable that they should prefer Browning to Tennyson. For in Tennyson, even when there was not uneasiness, there was doubt; and belief in the ultimate goodness of things, in the worth-whileness of life, shines with a more subdued light in the author of *Crossing the Bar* than in the author of *Prospice* or the *Epilogue to Asolando*. An obituary notice of Tennyson praising his adherence to the accepted moral standards and religious beliefs speaks of his " wistful yet persistent faith in God in Duty and in Immortal Love." And once more, " It is only moral fidelity, well-disciplined conduct and rightly ordered life that can be the parents of that divine sensitiveness to eternal verities which opens up the avenues of the mind to spiritual assurance, though not to intellectual certainty." Now, Britannia felt herself safer with intellectual certainty than with wistful faith.

These were days in which anyone who proclaimed that he did not read Browning, or that he disliked him, ran the risk of being branded as an uneducated person or, worse, an eccentric. But perhaps it was even more dangerous to admire him too much, for that was to be an intellectual prig. These opinions are very clearly recorded in the periodical literature

5

of the age. There was praise and blame in most of the articles in reviews. The *Edinburgh*, it is true, had learnt nothing and forgotten nothing. " His scholarship was imperfect, and he was insensible to the niceties of language and composition . . . involved parentheses—obscure periphrases . . . whimsical experiments in metre . . . extravagant combinations of rhyme." And again, " Mr. Browning's characters are for the most part branded with depravity and guilt." Is it fanciful to hear in such language nothing more than an echo of the voice of the Fifties ? The echo persists elsewhere—in the *Athenæum*, for instance, whose reviewer, in tones of the sincerest praise, exclaims : " In his depicting of love, he is pre-eminently the gentleman." Speaking generally, it would seem that Browning's obscurity and the harshness of his verse, the aridity and involution of most of his later work—all this was pronounced blameworthy. But these faults were judged to have been redeemed by the profundity of his thought, by his optimism, his courage and sometimes (though the point is by no means always made) by his keen insight into the minds of men. They praised " a deep one-ness in his teaching," his " splendid courage and confidence," his " priceless gems of thought too roughly set," his " indomitable —not exactly optimism, but determination to make and find life worth living," his " marvellous vigour of intellect," his " power of delivering an electric shock."

The obituary notices of the poet do not fail to remark that, great as his reputation was, the number of his readers—of his faithful readers—was small in comparison with the readers of Tennyson. " For a large majority of the English reading public," said

one review, " this kingly poet remains a name only."
This fact had not escaped Dr. Furnivall, and in his
enthusiasm he determined to take steps to right the
wrong.   Hence the Browning Society of London.
That Society must occupy our attention for a while
because of the very important influence it had upon
Browning's reputation.   The period of its fullest
activity was the Eighties, but it survived on through
the first few years of the next decade.   The marvel
is that it did not expire sooner from the shafts of
ridicule aimed at it from all sides.   Yet anyone who
will take the trouble to discover what the Society
was and what it aimed at, will be struck by the un-
fairness of the attacks upon it.   The fact is that even
in its lifetime very few people outside the Society
knew much about it.   The idea spread that it con-
sisted of people who, moved by intellectual prig-
gishness and conceit, looked upon themselves as an
élite, possessing, they alone, the key to Browning's
obscurities and taking a perverse delight in analysing
the difficulties of *Sordello* and *Fifine at the Fair*.
Thus Andrew Lang wrote that they praised
Browning's poetry " chiefly because they believe
that they alone understand it."   The *London Quarterly* cried, " the wicked world resents their tone of
superiority."   The *Athenæum* blamed their " perverse ingenuity," and the *Saturday Review* pictured
them as engaged in inventing " some far-fetched
apologies for a strange, though not a poetical,
licence."
    Now, there is no evidence that the members of the
Society were " wild " or that they assumed a tone
of superiority, or claimed to be the only people who
understood Browning.   Far from being wild, they
were, for the most part, respectable middle-class

people with a sprinkling of a few distinguished names
—Bishop Westcott, Dr. Furnivall, George Bernard
Shaw. They did not put on superior airs. They
came together to study Browning's works and to
encourage a wider reading of them. They felt that
without serious and attentive study it was impossible
to gather in what Browning had to give, and they
hoped, by working together, to have mutual help in
this serious and attentive study. For they believed
that what Browning had to give them was not an
occasion for mutual admiration accompanied by
cigarettes and cocktails, but the very word of life.
Nor did they believe that they alone could interpret
Browning to the rest of the world. They by no
means confined their efforts to elucidating obscurities. Typical titles of lectures and papers are
" Browning's Treatment of Parenthood," " The
Religious Teaching of Robert Browning," " The
Wife-Love and Friend-Love of Robert Browning."
They listened to Mr. (afterwards Sir) Walter Raleigh,
Arthur Symons, W. M. Rossetti, Professor Bury,
Professor Herford. There is no more reason for
imputing conceit and presumption to them than to
any set of people who have ever met to listen to
discourse on poetry in Bloomsbury or Balham, in
Chelsea or in Palmer's Green. No doubt, since
they were human, their motives were mixed, but on
the whole it seems fairest to think of them as a group
of some two hundred earnest, not particularly distinguished, people who were quite sincere lovers
of Browning and were not gifted with enough
sensibility or imaginative sympathy to perceive that,
far from drawing more people to his poetry, they
were tending to make him ridiculous. Browning
thought that they had actually increased the sale of

his works : yet it is difficult to believe that this was so.

But let us return to the impulsive Dr. Furnivall. The story of his relations with Browning and with the Society is astounding and might lead anyone who was ignorant of his work in other fields and his happier relations with those whom he tried to serve to think that he was engaged in a profoundly subtle plot to ruin the poet's reputation. The late Sir Edmund Gosse once said, " Furnivall did not hate Browning, but he loved him with a *deadly* love." When Furnivall was discussing the formation of a Browning Society with a certain Miss Hickey (to whom, by a curious coincidence, the same idea had occurred quite independently), the latter timidly suggested that Browning might not approve of the scheme. Furnivall, not in any way perturbed by this suggestion, declared that he would proceed with his plan even if the poet disapproved. He wrote a paper for the Society in which he discussed Browning's ancestry. For the theory that Browning had negro blood in his veins he could find no certain proof : with keener regret he had to abandon the idea that he was partly Jewish : but he triumphantly demonstrated that the founder of the family was a butler. He raked out from the family records and held up with great glee for the inspection of the public the story of a breach of promise case in which Browning's father had been mixed up. He wrote a whole paper taken up with a grammatical analysis of the Invocation in *The Ring and the Book*—" O lyric Love . . ."

With such auspices did the Society begin its career. Of Browning's relations with the Society more may fall to be said in another place. They show up in a very favourable light his tact, his modesty, his discretion and his sense of humour.

Three of the most prominent members of the Society were J. T. Nettleship, Mrs. Orr and Dr. Berdoe, each of whom produced books still fairly widely read. Mrs. Orr's life of the poet, in its latest edition revised by Sir F. G. Kenyon, still deserves to be considered the standard biography. Of more immediate interest in this context is her *Handbook*, written, as she herself says, at the request of the Browning Society, which in 1884[1] contributed £45 towards the expenses of publication. It was favourably, though not enthusiastically, received by the press, and ran into many editions. Nettleship's *Essays and Thoughts* was a much earlier work, first published in 1868. It was, however, considerably enlarged in subsequent editions, and included papers read to the Browning Society. Dr. Berdoe also read papers to the Society and compiled a Browning Encyclopædia.

None of these three books is likely to survive by virtue of literary merit or critical illumination, but in their day they have had some influence, and since they do reflect a particular attitude to Browning characteristic of the end of the last century, they cannot be passed over. Of Berdoe's *Encyclopædia* it is not necessary to say much. The author had read his poet frequently and faithfully, but few people who can claim to be educated will stand in need of his *Encyclopædia*, and though there are passages in it full of unintentional humour, they are hardly worth the labour of searching out. One instance will suffice. Berdoe is explaining the poem *Parting at Morning* :

[1] The book was published in 1885.

Round the cape of a sudden came the sea,
And the sun looked over the mountain's rim :
And straight was a path of gold for him,
And the need of a world of men for me.

This is the explanation : " In the sequel the rising
sun calls men to work : the man of the poem
to work of a lucrative character ; and excites in the
woman (if we interpret the slightly obscure line
correctly) a desire for more society than the seaside
home affords."

J. T. Nettleship was an artist—an animal painter.
It may seem strange in this day that a member of the
Browning Society should have been a contributor to
The Yellow Book—but Nettleship's drawing, " Head
of Minos," did not appear until the days when *The
Yellow Book* had almost lost its colour. On the
other hand, a surviving member of the Society has
described Nettleship as " a quiescent member."
Indeed, on one occasion he went so far as to sympathise with the poet upon the embarrassment which
the existence of the Society must cause him. His
book in its final form contains twenty-nine essays
in addition to the Introduction and the " Last
Words." They vary widely from mediocrity re-
lieved by occasional flashes of real insight to sheer
stupidity. The main object of the studies is to
" evolve thoughts " rather than " to trace beauties or
faults of construction," to " discover lessons for
actual life " rather than " to examine historical
evidences." A characteristic passage is this : " One
may fairly presume that in giving us portraits of
selfish love, the poet intended us to see . . . that
the selfishness of it is in general a fatal drawback to
its influence as a useful thing." Nettleship,
indeed, judged by the standard of to-day—and, in

justice to the past, one must add, judged by the standards of Matthew Arnold and of Pater—was ill equipped for the work of a literary critic. For instance, if he was widely read in English and in foreign literature, he was unable or unwilling to make use of that reading. But he is found wanting in other fundamental qualities also. There should be in the critic a sense of proportion—something of its nature intuitive—which would have prevented Nettleship from committing the absurdities of his essays on *Saul* and *Childe Roland*. It has been noted that Nettleship's aim was " to evolve thoughts " and " discover lessons for actual life "—that is, to attempt to unfold the implications for conduct contained in Browning's poems. Consider the result in the case of *Saul*.

" Here are two human creatures, the one, sunk far down out of the empyræan, where life, the choragus, leads the chorus of humanity, to the rhythm of a voiceless melody in a perpetual dance of dazzling light ; and another who has stooped, bidden by God, down from that empyræan, to plunge into the black slough in which, too inert and dead for any effort at escape, the lost man wallows silently. From the utmost verge of that black slough, from the far away gate of hell at which he lies, obstinately marrowless, so stupidly negative that even hell's king scorns to open and welcome him, who can bring him back ? Can David, so white and joyous, so glowing with the life dance ? Let us see."

This is the very acme of fatuity. It was this sort of thing which provoked the *National Observer's* parody :

" God made Mr. Browning a Fisher of sins ; he trolls his lay and lo ! he brings up from the ooze of the infinite heart of man some blue mysterious lobster-like sin, boils it in the massy iron alembic of his imagination and exhibits it blushing scarlet for shame in the white light of his wife's morality."

But it is not the silliness of the thought which constitutes the chief offence of the passage—it is rather the entire misunderstanding of the whole purpose of the poem.   The misunderstanding arises, clearly, from Nettleship's determination that the poem shall at all costs be shown to have a moral— " For us of to-day, then," he asks, " what is the lesson which the poet would teach ? "   And the poet himself had more than once answered such questions —his answer is clear to read in the title of the book— *Dramatic Romances and Lyrics*.   But even if that answer seemed doubtful to a critic in the case of *Saul*, in the case of another poem it was plain enough. Dr. Furnivall put it on record that three separate times he had asked Browning whether there was any hidden or underlying meaning in *Childe Roland*, and every time Browning had answered " No."   But even this did not prevent Nettleship from writing a paper on *Childe Roland* in which he finds " a second meaning "—" That ' round squat turret . . . without counterpart in the whole world '—may it not be some strange, seemingly fantastic end, which men have proposed to themselves ere now, as the one end which had in it the truth and was of power to set the world free and make it happy ? "   And so on through eighteen pages of close print.   Nettleship was well aware of what he was doing, but he set out to justify himself by quoting George Eliot : " The

words of genius bear a wider meaning than the
thought which prompted them." The impression
made by this essay upon Browning himself is worth
noting here. A surviving member of the Browning
Society has told the writer that he well remembers
visiting the poet one Sunday morning and bringing
for his perusal the copy of the *Browning Society
Papers* which contained Nettleship's essay. Browning, after reading the paper, laughed heartily and
remarked that he supposed it was there in the poem,
though he hadn't known it when he wrote it ! Upon
which the only comment is that not many poets would
have been provoked to laughter by such treatment. But there is a point here which will be dealt
with presently when the attitude of Browning
towards his critics is being considered.

That Nettleship in his explanations of various
poems or passages in poems should very often have
been wrong is in itself unimportant, but it is worth
pausing to consider the kind of mistake of which he
was guilty. It will be convenient to take as an
example his comment on *Fifine at the Fair*. Two
points must be brought out sharply. First, as we
should expect, Nettleship treats the whole thing as
a long-drawn-out lesson in conduct. Secondly, since
Browning had acknowledged that there was an
element of sophistry in the poem, Nettleship in his
paraphrase employs three signs by which to distinguish those parts which seem to him sophistical,
those which contain a mixture of truth and sophistry,
and those which are true. It need hardly be said
that, having approached the poem with the declared
intention of finding in it a moral and of marking off
sophistry and truth, he was exposed to a temptation,
which in the event proved irresistible, to give a

strained interpretation to many passages. Here is
an example. In stanza xvi the Don Juan of the
poem makes a simple statement. " I ask," he says,
" but to understand

> The acknowledged victory of whom I call my queen,
> Sexless and bloodless sprite : though mischievous and mean,
> Yet free and flower like too, with loveliness for law
> And self sustainment made morality."

There is nothing in those lines (taken in their context) which could be called obscure. Don Juan is
attracted by those things in gipsy-life which the
more respectable part of the community call lawless.
He wants to analyse this attraction—to discover why
this creature Fifine—sexless, bloodless, mischievous,
mean—attracts him. Nettleship's actual paraphrase
of the lines quoted, though not illuminating, is not
wide of the mark : and yet he has labelled the passage sophistry. Why ? Presumably because he did
not like to think that Browning could be attracted
by an immoral person like Fifine—or perhaps, more
generally, that he could feel the attraction of a
Bohemian existence—that he was capable of taking
sides with the Bohemian against the bourgeois.

Still more serious, however, is Nettleship's entire
misunderstanding of one of the most important
passages in the whole poem. In that passage is
embodied an interesting philosophy, poles asunder
from what is accepted as characteristic of Browning's
point of view. It occurs in stanza cxxviii, and again
the meaning is not obscure. The claim that there is a
soul or spiritual power controlling the universe is
supported in this passage by just the fact that man's
soul is not exalted by such a belief, finds no triumph
in it—only submission, since the soul of the in-

dividual can take no pride in acknowledging that another soul plays master everywhere. Now, in Nettleship's paraphrase this passage is marked as containing neither sophistry, nor a mixture of truth and sophistry, but the very truth. But before receiving it as true he has misinterpreted it. He says in his paraphrase what Don Juan in the poem neither says nor implies, that " the ultimate truth " learned by the soul is " the approach of the body's death," and that in this thought " there is no cause for pride, for this truth merely warns the soul its right of rule will go and another soul succeeding it must be master in future." This is not in the poem. The ultimate truth of which Don Juan is speaking is not the approach of the body's death but the existence of an all-controlling spirit. The passage as transfigured or mutilated by Nettleship would not be found a stumbling-block by anyone and is not out of line with orthodox Christian teaching—whereas what Don Juan really did utter was a characteristic pagan thought.

But the whole passage is so interesting both in itself and because of its strange reaction upon a typical interpreter like Nettleship, that there is no excuse needed for dwelling upon it a little longer. The argument of the passage is based upon an analogy between body and soul. The bodily organism in its evolution through immensely long periods takes to itself—assimilates—whatever promotes its well-being, its own personal interests. It knows what it wants—it never makes a mistake. In a similar kind of way (but with one hugely important difference) the soul or mind selects among opinions or beliefs those which it thinks most likely to make it happy—which in practice means, those

most flattering to its pride. The difference between
the body and the mind of the individual is that the
mind makes mistakes. The opinions which it has
selected because they flatter its pride have no basis
in reality. If, then, we do ever find that the mind
accepts an opinion or belief which does not make it
happier and does not flatter its sense of self-import-
ance, we can only suppose that there is some special
property in the conception which compels accept-
ance, however reluctant the mind may be. And
this property can be none other than truth. The
whole passage, from one point of view, is an expression of a simple thought, that of what we call truths,
the disagreeable ones are likely to be the truest.
We cannot know for certain what mark Nettleship
would have put against this passage if he had read it
aright, but it is difficult to believe that he would have
called it the very truth without immediately adding
a long footnote to explain that all really was right with
the world.

One of the essays in Nettleship's *Studies* is a review
of Mrs. Sutherland Orr's *Handbook*. It begins with
these words :

" If the Browning Societies had done nothing else
—and much sterling work has been evoked by them
—we should be grateful to them for having evoked
Mrs. Orr's handbook. . . . It is clear, exhaustive
within its limits, and authentic throughout." . . .

Other critics also spoke in its favour, but the *London
Quarterly* strongly disapproved ; and the main
ground of disapproval is that the author mis-
represented Browning's views. And thus at the
moment of the book's appearance we find that on

the one hand a reviewer who was well acquainted
with the writer and with Browning describes it as
authentic, while another reviewer condemns it for
traducing the poet's thought. And, indeed, the
question of the authenticity of the book is one of the
minor puzzles of literary history.

Let us first consider the facts of the situation as far
as they are known. Mrs. Orr was a sister of Sir
Frederic Leighton. Her health was weak, and in
particular she suffered from defective eyesight.
That the friendship between herself and Browning
can be described as intimate there is little doubt.
She first made the acquaintance of Browning and
Mrs. Browning in Paris in 1855. In later years
Browning used to read to her twice a week. According to Thomas Hardy, some of Browning's friends
believed " that there was something tender between
Mrs. Orr and Browning. ' Why don't they settle
it ? ' said Mrs. Proctor.'' But others who also knew
both the poet and his interpreter declare that on his
side, at any rate, there was never anything " tender."
There, however, is a point which must be left to the
biographers. What concerns us is this question—
from so close a friendship, what could we deduce as
to the authenticity of the *Handbook* ? It seems impossible that there should not have been frequent
discussions of the poet's more difficult passages.
And, indeed, we know that there were discussions—
the preface to the second edition says : " By Mr.
Browning's desire, I have corrected two mistakes."
One of these was " a misreading of an historical
allusion in *The Statue and the Bust*." And again
she says, " I should have stated in my first Preface
. . . that I owe to Mr. Browning's kindness all the
additional matter which my own reading could not

supply . . ." and this edition contains the signed notes by the poet. The case for authenticity seems complete, and it is hardly necessary to add this passage from the diary of Mary Gladstone (Mrs. Drew: " He (Browning) told me about Mrs. Sutherland Orr (Leighton's sister), and what an astonishing interpretation of him was her handbook."

But immediately one turns to the *Handbook* itself, all sorts of difficulties crop up. Take, for instance, this very comment on *The Statue and the Bust*, certain details in which Browning himself had taken the trouble to correct. " He (Browning) leaves the bust in the region of fancy, by stating that it no longer exists," says Mrs. Orr, " but he tells us that it was executed in ' Della Robbia ' ware." The meaning of the sentence is not very clear at first sight, but when one looks at it carefully it seems able to mean only this : " Browning tells us that the bust is no longer there, and so we have to resort to our own fancy to supply a picture of it." That is to say, if you go to Florence you will find that the bust has disappeared, as, indeed, Browning says it has. The only clue which Browning gives, by which we can judge what the bust looked like, is that it was executed in " Della Robbia " ware. Mrs. Orr leaves the reader quite clear on one point—that there *was* a bust once in the place, but that it is no longer there. But we happen to know—for Hardy has left on record the poet's own words—that Browning invented the bust, that it never existed, and that Browning knew that it never existed. How then, if he put Mrs. Orr right on one historical error in the poem, did he come to leave this other uncorrected ? If Mrs. Orr's testimony that the poet read her interpretation were not enough, we have other evidence on the

point.   Mr. T. J. Wise once forwarded to Browning
a letter from a reader who had been puzzled by
something in the poem.   Browning in his reply
to Mr. Wise remarked that he had looked up
Mrs. Orr's *Handbook* to see what she had to say on
the point.

But here is something even more bewildering.
The poem *Another Way of Love* has puzzled many
readers.   Consider the last stanza :

> And after, for pastime,
>   If June be refulgent
> With flowers in completeness,
>   All petals, no prickles,
>   Delicious as trickles
> Of wine poured at mass-time,—
>   And choose one indulgent
>   To redness and sweetness :
> Or if with experience of man and of spider,
> June use my June—lightning, the strong insect-ridder,
> And stop the fresh film-work,—why, June will consider.

Which Mrs. Orr paraphrases thus : " She reminds
him, however, that June may repair her bower,
which his hand has rifled, and the next time consider
which of the two courses she prefers : to bestow her
flowers on one who will accept their sweetness, or
use her lightnings to kill the spider who is weaving
his films about them."   The lady, we see, has dis-
missed one lover and is debating with herself how she
will behave next time—i.e. when next some lover
sues.   But it so happens that Browning had himself
given an explanation of the stanza.   Here it is.
" The lady, a passionate Italian, means, ' Whether I
shall find a new lover and bestow on him all that you
despise, and even more,—forgetting all else ; or
whether I shall not rather bethink myself of taking
a thorough revenge on you—that is for after-con-

sideration : you are not ' out of the wood ' yet."
Now, the poem thus understood has an immeasur-
ably greater dramatic value than as interpreted by
Mrs. Orr : in fact, Mrs. Orr's interpretation creates
a veritable anti-climax in the poem and makes
almost a bathos of its ending. Once more we
are left wondering why Browning took no notice
of this mutilation.

We have seen Dr. Berdoe's interpretation of
Parting at Morning. And it so happens that Browning himself gave the authentic interpretation for the
benefit of " The Day's End Club " of Exeter. The
last line of the poem runs :

> And the need of a world of men for me,

and Browning writes : " It is his confession (the
confession of the speaker in the poem) of how fleeting
is the belief (implied in the first part [1]) that such
raptures are self-sufficient and enduring—as for the
time they appear." Now, Browning wrote this
answer in 1889, and he did not refer his inquirers to
Mrs. Orr's *Handbook*, though that was already in its
third edition. Had the " Day's End Club " con-
sulted Mrs. Orr ? It is not impossible, for Mrs.
Orr's comment on the poem does not give much
help—" *Parting at Morning* asserts the need of
' men ' and their ' world ' which is born again with
the sunshine." But Browning, we have seen, set
a high value on the *Handbook*, and on at least one
occasion looked to see whether a particular difficulty
referred to him by a correspondent had been solved
by Mrs. Orr. It might be expected that on this
occasion he would have followed the same course.

---

[1] I.e. in *Meeting at Night*.

6

In that case he would hardly have failed to communicate with Mrs. Orr, and she would have changed, i.e. expanded and altered, her comment in the next edition (which as a matter of fact appeared just before Browning's death). Nevertheless, many circumstances can be imagined which would explain that omission. The point is that in this discrepancy between Browning's explanation and Mrs. Orr's we have another argument against the complete authenticity of the *Handbook*.

It is very probable that Mrs. Orr's *Handbook* has ceased to be important—even though certainly it is still in fairly wide use. The question of its authenticity need not have delayed us, but that Mrs. Orr's work has to be considered as in some degree characteristic of her age. She takes up a quite definite attitude, in her *Handbook*, towards Browning's poetry—very much the same attitude as Nettleship. If then the authenticity of the book could be established, we should have to accept her account of the significance of Browning's work as being the poet's own account.

But from what has already been said it is clear that the *Handbook* need by no means be regarded as infallible. If serious discrepancies occur between the *Handbook* and the Poems, the problem will be for the reader of to-day, not to find some way of reconciling his reading with Mrs. Orr's, but to understand how it came about that Browning openly praised a book which gives demonstrably wrong interpretations of his work. The treatment of that problem is reserved for a later chapter, and what remains to be done here is to give examples of such discrepancies, selecting for this purpose interpretations by Mrs. Orr which seem characteristic of a whole body of opinion rather than individual to herself.

A minor point may be noticed first. Browning enjoyed then—and still in many quarters enjoys— a reputation for wide and deep erudition. When this erudition is tested it is found that its width is more considerable than its depth, but in the Nineties it had not been subjected to tests except in connection with his translations from the Greek. Mrs. Orr, speaking of *Sordello*, says that Browning had prepared himself by studying all the chronicles of that period of Italian history which the British Museum supplied : " and we may be sure that every event he alluded to as historical is so in spirit, if not in the letter." Now, the fact is that a careful study of the historicity of *Sordello* will show that Mrs. Orr was wrong, and overrated the accuracy of the poem—in the spirit as well as in the letter. This ascription of immense learning to the poet is of importance because beyond question it supported his authority as a thinker upon all subjects.

But much more important is the particular angle from which Mrs. Orr looks at the whole of the poet's work. She sees it as a body of ethical doctrine and as the expression of religious beliefs. While the poet was proclaiming from the housetops that his work was essentially dramatic—the utterances of imaginary persons and not of himself—in other words, that he was a psychologist—Mrs. Orr was telling the man in the street that Browning was a moral teacher. Of *Sordello* she says, " The intended lesson of the story is distinctly enforced in the last scene," whereas if we turn to the text we find that Browning does not seek a lesson to be drawn from Sordello's life, but a psychological explanation of

Sordello's failure. " What made the secret of his
past despair ? " asks Browning : he does not go on
to ask, " What lesson can we learn from the secret
of his past despair ? " In exactly the same way a
whole series of dramatic monologues are described
as " defences." For instance, *Fifine* is " a defence
of inconstancy, or of the right of experiment in
love " ; *Bishop Blougram*, " a defence of religious
conformity in those cases in which the doctrines to
which we conform exceed our powers of belief but
are not throughout opposed to them." But to this
rule of Mrs. Orr's there is one exception. She takes
Christmas Eve and *Easter Day* to be dramatic poems
and not lessons. Why ? Beyond question there
were readers of that day, there are readers in this day,
who cherish those two poems precisely because they
give expression to their own religious beliefs.
There may be two explanations of Mrs. Orr's willing-
ness to treat the two poems as dramatic and psychological—and both explanations may hold good. The
first is that Browning—as we know from Mrs.
Browning's letters—had expressly stated that these
two poems were not an expression of his own religious views. And the second is that the views
expressed in them could not be reconciled with Mrs.
Orr's own religious and philosophical views. For
the Christianity of the two poems, especially of
Easter Day, is largely orthodox, and Mrs. Orr was,
if not an agnostic, at any rate distinctly not an
orthodox Christian. Wherefore, if in reference to
any particular poem she can interpret the text as the
expression of some belief not orthodox, she will
assign to that poem a didactic purpose. If she fails
so to interpret it, the poem is described as dramatic.
She ascribes to Browning in her introduction the

belief that " Christ is a spiritual mystery far more than a definable or dogmatic fact." Now, in *Christmas Eve* Christ appears as a visible fact and the speaker ends the poem by declaring his adherence to the Christianity of the Nonconformist tabernacle. So again, when Mrs. Orr comments on *A Death in the Desert* she finds that Browning is expressing his own views in the words of Saint John in those passages in which Saint John maintains that doubt is the test of faith and its preserver. But the Christology of the poem is said (or implied) by her to be dramatic, and is represented as unsoundly based (and here we may notice a comment by Nettle-ship on the same poem, that it " goes no single step in the direction of proving Christ's divinity as a dogma "). The whole trend of Mrs. Orr's work, so far as it is occupied with Browning's religious views, is towards the suggestion that he did not hold the Christian faith. Actually there is a substantial body of evidence in favour of supposing that he did (see *The Life of Robert Browning*, W. Hall Griffin and H. C. Minchin, pp. 294 following).

In the attitude taken up towards Browning's work by the main body of reviewers of the Fifties we remarked a curious anomaly—this, namely, that they failed to recognise in Browning a thinker who was in many ways representative of the age. And again those of the more prominent men of letters who in the Nineties had anything to say or write about Browning seem to us of to-day curiously blind to things in him which one might expect them to have admired or execrated. Do we find the same thing in the Browning Society commentators—in the quiet and thoughtful people who read him in vicarages and in comfortable middle-class villas in the Nineties ? In a certain measure we do. It is necessary to recall what they wanted to find in Browning. They wanted a man with a consoling and strengthening message—a man who believed in men ; who believed that the world was not the creation of an Aristophanic God ; who could uphold the code of conduct traditional in British middle-class homes—and if one article in that code seemed more important than another (then as now), it was that which concerned marriage and inter-course of the sexes generally. They wanted to find that kind of man in Browning, and because they wanted to find, they found. But while Browning, there is no doubt, considered that marriage was the fit consummation of romantic love, holding in that with the Victorians, he differed in not looking upon their code as absolute or final ; and he could specu-late on ways and times in which it might break down. *The Statue and the Bust* is a speculation of this kind : it horrified the readers of the Fifties. They exagger-ated its importance : the Victorians of the Nineties probably underestimated it.

Consider for a moment one of the main themes of *The Ring and the Book*. That poem seems to our generation the work of " an infinitely respectable rebel," yet it was in certain ways calculated rudely to shock the doctor, the solicitor, the Dean, the school-master and the literary-minded ship-owner of the Nineties. Those people must surely have found it difficult to approve of a Pope who reserved his high-est praise for the woman who turned a sword against her husband's breast. " Thou," he says, addressing Pompilia :

> Thou, patient thus, could'st rise from law to law,
> The old to the new, promoted at one cry

O' the trump of God to the new service, not
To longer bear, but henceforth fight, be found
Sublime in new impatience with the foe !
Endure man and obey God : plant firm foot
On neck of man, tread man into the hell
Meet for him, and obey God all the more !

One is tempted to wander farther down that page because there is much in the thought there which seems to belong less to the years in which it was conceived—and the years in which it was praised—than to our own time.

How the fine ear felt full the first low word
" Value life, and preserve life for My sake ! "
Thou didst—how shall I say ?—receive so long
The standing ordinance of God on earth,
What wonder if the novel claim had clashed
With old requirement, seemed to supersede
Too much the customary law ?   But, brave,
Thou at first promptings of what I call God,
And fools call Nature, didst hear, comprehend,
Accept the obligation laid on thee,
Mother elect, to save the unborn child,
As brute and bird do, reptile and the fly,
Ay and, I nothing doubt, even tree, shrub, plant
And flower o' the field, all in a common pact
To worthily defend the trust of trusts,
Life from the Ever Living. . . .[1]

And that must have sounded strange, if she had been able to hear truly, to the lady who had just turned out of doors her housemaid who was carrying with her too evident signs of " an unfortunate affair " with the milkman.   And to less inhuman persons than this there must have been much to ponder over, if

[1] Mrs. Orr's paraphrase of all this passage in her *Handbook* is particularly significant.   Evidently she had learnt the value of the precept " Glissez, n'appuyez point "—" With Pompilia the right virtue is always employed for the good end.   She is submissive where only her own life is at stake ; brave when a life within her own calls on her for protection."

they ever connected this and like passages in *The Ring and the Book* with *The Statue and the Bust* and with *The Flight of the Duchess*. As for *Fifine*, enough has already been said to show how sorely this perplexed the Browningites, and what desperate measures they took to explain it all away.

CHAPTER V

THE NINETEEN-TWENTIES

THE difficulty every critic meets of picking out what is characteristic of the poetical thought of a given age naturally becomes greater the nearer that age is to his own. It is enormous in the case of the Nineteen-twenties, not only because it is difficult for anyone to know what a forest is like as a whole when he is in the middle of it, but because this particular forest is so vast and contains so many different kinds of vegetation. It seems incredible that in this country any age could have shown more violently contrasted poetry than that of Sir Henry Newbolt and that of Miss Edith Sitwell or more violently contrasted critical methods than those of Professor Elton and those of Mr. I. A. Richards. And between these extremes and extending, so to speak, far and wide on each side of the line which joins them are innumerable gradations of types of poetic thought. Selection was therefore necessary for the purposes of the present chapter, and the process of selecting was inevitably determined by the personal limitations of the selector. Even when, fearfully and after long thought, a certain field had been marked out, the classifying and analysing of what it contained brought a multitude of new dangers. For the final result nothing is claimed except that certain tendencies presently to be named were real tendencies, even though the origin of them and the weight to be attached to them might fairly

be disputed.   Thus there is no doubt that the tone
of that body of poetry which revealed a general outlook upon life was pessimistic rather than optimistic,
but how far this may have been due to the influence
of Hardy, to the discoveries and speculations of
science, or to a number of causes operating to produce in the whole community a feeling of disillusionment and bitterness, is a problem on which no one
can yet speak with authority.   Again, poets writing in
that decade did on the whole attach a higher value
than their predecessors to simplicity of language, to
directness of expression and to conciseness.   It is
open to discuss how far that simplicity is genuine, and
whether it was or was not successful in its reaction
against the more opulent and heavily laden language
of the Victorians.   Once more, no one nowadays
reads *The Ring and the Book*, and few poems are
printed which cover more than one page of a book.
Is this due to a weakness—for instance, are we less
strong of heart and shorter of breath than Robert
Browning?—or is it all to the good, because the
particular things that have to be said now must be
said shortly or not at all ?

To questions of this sort—though not necessarily
to these particular questions—some kind of answer
will be offered.   How precarious that answer is no
one knows better than the writer.   But something
will have been gained which may help forward the
general endeavour of this study, if the mere enumera-
tion of important influences operating in the decade
of the Twenties does not prove to have been quite
unreliable.

During the first few years of the new century the
output of books and articles on Browning continued
in great volume.   But after Mr. Chesterton's con-

tribution to the *English Men of Letters* series, the
stream began to shrink rapidly, and by 1910 or there-
abouts was reduced to a mere trickle. The centen-
ary of the poet's birth brought, in 1912, a valuable
contribution to criticism in the shape of Henry
James's article in the *Quarterly Review*; and in
Professor Elton's *Survey*, published in 1920, the
treatment of Browning is no less wise, thorough and
sympathetic than that which he accords to any other
Victorian.

Browning continues to be read, but there is no
Browning Society. Except by examination candi-
dates, not very much is written about his poetry, and
that little is not whole-hearted in praise. To compare him with Tennyson—an initiatory ceremony in
the literary salons of the Nineties—is now a purely
academic exercise. The editor of any review of
good standing would not trouble to read beyond the
title of a manuscript on " The Philosophy of Robert
Browning " or " Robert Browning's Views on
Parenthood " or " Browning's Physicians." Not
that the ghost of the Browning Society is entirely
laid, though its corpse has been all but half a century
in the tomb. It speaks in a passage like this, taken
from a book published in 1923. The reference is
to the tenth stanza of *Abt Vogler* (" All we have
willed or hoped . . .") :

" Surely this is an immense declaration ! One
asks oneself, is it true ? And if it is true, is it so
only for the intellectual giant and the genius ?
Robert Browning asserts it as a truth for all !
God is eternal ! It is power in man, derived
from the Divine itself, and we have no gauge by
which to measure its relative value since, all unknown to her, the widow's farthing headed that

memorable subscription list two thousand years
ago.''

While Browning continues to be read and enjoyed
by the inarticulate many, the attitude of the reviews
of our day has been not always too friendly. Not that
all critics without exception condemn him. Most
of them are indifferent rather than hostile. Others,
for instance Mr. F. L. Lucas, find much to praise,
even if there is still more that they hate. A few
praise him, not without reserve, but with the reserva-
tions implied rather than expressed. Mr. Osbert
Burdett, the latest biographer of the Brownings,
reminds himself that '' Browning is the only modern
poet whose range, humanity, humour, mastery of
language and variety of gifts invited comparison with
Shakespeare.''

Browning is a Victorian, and there has been in the
present century a strong reaction against the
Victorians. But it is interesting to note that the
special kind of hostility which characterises the
attitude of some contemporary critics had found
expression before the anti-Victorian reaction set in.
This new hostility is directed not so much against
those peculiarities of style—e.g. harshness of verse,
obscurity, language, involution of thought—which
had angered the critics of the Eighteen-fifties and
Eighteen-sixties as against Browning's point of
view, his attitude towards life. Here is an example
taken from one of the earliest specimens of the new
criticism (*Browning for Beginners*, by the Reverend T.
Rain). The critic, who has many things to say in
praise of the poet, cannot stomach his optimism.
He contrasts the optimism and idealism of
Browning with the despair and realism of Maxim

Gorki, from whom he quotes: " I have come from below, from the nethermost ground of life, where is nought but sludge and muck. . . . I am the truthful voice of life, the harsh cry of those who still abide down there and who have let me come up to bear witness to their sufferings." Mr. Rain comments :

" Would Browning have listened to such a voice ? Would he even have heard it, this shriek of wildness and despair ? I doubt if he would. His art so absorbed him that he had no time to look on commonplace life, far less lay its grim facts to heart. . . . Full well Browning knows there are victims. But the knowledge of this does not seem to disturb him ; he nowhere writes as a man whom the thought of it has stricken to the heart ; contriving to forget, he goes upon his way, cheerily singing—

> "' God's in His Heaven,
> All's right with the world.' "

And a little further comes this : " Sometimes . . . we lose patience and blaspheme. We incline to bid him ' shut up.' "

The nature and extent of the reaction against Browning is the main subject of this chapter, but, as in other chapters, so here it has been thought well to begin by noting in a general way some of the main tendencies exhibited by poetry as it developed in the Nineteen-twenties. And the three tendencies which are to be discussed here are these : First, a pessimistic trend of thought, strongly influenced by the philosophical implications which appeared to underlie the theories and suggestions of men of science ; secondly, a revolt against analytic reason (logic)— or rather a new manifestation of a revolt, the beginnings of which, so far as poetry is concerned, must be dated at least as far back as the beginnings of the Romantic Movement ; thirdly, a movement proceeding in an exactly opposite direction from the last, and on that account to be referred to as Neo-Rationalism or Neo-Classicism.

By definition a pessimist is a man who has had to live with an optimist. Browning was an optimist with whom poets and critics had been living for upwards of half a century, so that the reaction against him was to be expected and may have been necessary. And, as we have already suggested, it is part of the general reaction against the whole point of view of the Victorian age. We have already noted that the whole manner of life of the Victorians has been held up to ridicule—their love of mahogany, horsehair, candelabra, crinolines ; the prudery which made them drape piano legs and call trousers " indispensables " ; their empty, lifeless idealism, their self-interest disguised as righteousness—in a word, their mixture of hypocrisy, cunning and obtuseness. A smug and stuffy age. That condemnation was not invented in the Twenties ; it was invented by Mr. G. B. Shaw,[1] and the later decade accepted with its many minds one man's thesis and worked it out in detail. In this minutely particularised indictment of the Victorians the accusation of obtuseness is, for the moment, best worth examining. The Victorians, it is said, were wilfully blind to the evils which beset them. By dint of repetition they had convinced themselves that all was for the best in the best of all possible societies—and the most characteristic expression, the most frequently quoted expression of that obtuseness, is—

---

[1] A claim might be put in for Samuel Butler.

> God's in His Heaven,
> All's right with the world.

Whence it follows we might expect that Browning would be singled out for attack in any reaction towards a pessimistic point of view.

Such a reaction has taken place. Of all the names of poets associated with the swing-over to pessimism, none is greater than that of Thomas Hardy. Not that he himself would admit that he was a pessimist. He even claimed to be a meliorist. That seems strange, even if we allow on reflection that he was not in the strict sense of the word a pessimist—that is to say, he had not formed for himself a systematic philosophy of the type named pessimist. In the looser sense of the word he was a pessimist, because the view of life and of man's nature reflected in his poetry is full of the darkest gloom. It is worth considering certain points in his view of life, because he has so strongly influenced modern poetry.

Careful though Hardy was to disavow a systematic philosophy, there do exist very close resemblances between his attitude—if we may use no more precise word than that—and the philosophy of Schopenhauer, resemblances, indeed, hardly less striking than those between Browning's attitude and Christian philosophy. It is not that Hardy borrowed his point of view or attitude from Schopenhauer, or that he grew up with Schopenhauer as Browning grew up with the Bible. There is a parallel to be drawn between Hardy and Mr. Shaw. Mr. Shaw's attitude in his *Quintessence of Ibsenism* has analogies with the philosophy of Nietzsche in spite of the fact that, when the *Quintessence* was written, its author had not read Nietzsche. So also Hardy was, we might almost say, a Schopenhauerian pessimist before he

had read Schopenhauer. And yet it is certain that
he did at one time or another study Schopenhauer,
and from that point onward the philosopher's
influence on the poet was direct and considerable.
The total effect which issued in his poems may
perhaps be summed up by saying that he conceived
of man as a thing of nought, an infinitesimal point
against the stupendous background of the universe.
Sometimes man is represented as wholly pre-
determined in all his actions, unable to choose between this or that. Yet this predetermination must
not be taken as implying a reasoned plan in the
working out of history. Then, as for God, if there
is any God, he has forgotten earth and its inhabit-
ants—and this perhaps through man's fault ; man
may have severed himself from God. Or yet again
God is perhaps created by man in his own image—
a projection of himself designed to " ease his loaded
heart." Dethrone the man-created God, and what
is left is no more than a blind, listless Will which
knows nothing of pity or beauty. Yet in this point
of view—all the more because it is not a philosophy—
there are inconsistencies. Though anything like a
reasoned plan is excluded, yet the listless Will works
according to rote. Again, there is even—not indeed
a gleam of hope, but something like a vague stain
in one region of Hardy's dark sky. " Perhaps," he
says to the Will—

> Perhaps thy ancient rote-restricted ways
>   Thy ripening rule transcends ;
> That listless effort tends
> To grow percipient with advance of days,
>   And with percipience mends.

And there are traces of an uneasy feeling concerning the reality of the time process which, had Hardy

been philosophising, would have forced him to reconsider his conception of the Will and its workings. For an instance, take this from *The Absolute Explains*, the date of which is 1922 :

> Know, time is toothless, seen all through ;
>   The Present, that men but see,
> Is phasmal : since in a sane purview
>   All things were shaped to be
>   Eternally.
>
> Your " Now " is just a gleam, a glide
>   Across your gazing sense :
> With me, " Past," " Future," ever abide,
>   They come not, go not, whence
>   They are never hence.
>   .   .   .   .   .
> In fine, Time is a mock—yea, such !
>   As he might well confess :
> Yet hath he been believed in much,
>   Though lately, under stress
>   Of Science, less.

Hardy, then, comes in—or perhaps it would be more correct to say, was invoked—to lend strength to the anti-Victorian tendency of the new century, and in particular to the tendency to react from Victorian optimism and belief in progress. But there have been, of course, many other influences at work to shape the literary thinking of our day. The last line of the poem just quoted reminds us that science has been a most powerful influence. It is worth noting a significant difference in the attitude towards science of poets in our day and in earlier times. Tennyson, we know, studied certain branches of science, not, indeed, with profound seriousness, but systematically. It is scarcely to be believed that any poet of our own day has relatively the same knowledge of contemporary developments in science

7

as Tennyson had in his earlier years. The reason is simple—there is infinitely more to study in every branch of science. Nevertheless, the poet can form for himself a notion of the direction in which scientific thought is moving. He has not enough special knowledge or technical equipment to read what the scientists write for other scientists, but he can be made aware through *œuvres de vulgarisation* of certain consequences for our view concerning man's life and destiny and concerning the nature of his understanding and his emotions, which seem to flow from the researches of the scientist. And he may borrow—he does not infrequently borrow— some of the language of the scientist—astronomer, chemist, physicist, biologist, psychologist. Lastly, his understanding and knowledge of what is being done varies from science to science. For example, Freud is—or seems—easier to assimilate than Einstein.

Though it is perilous work to try to measure the influence thus exercised by science upon poetical thought in this day, the task cannot be wholly shirked. One or two manifestations of that influence must be mentioned in the hope that they may be accepted as significant. Perhaps we might conveniently begin with the astronomer, because, for one thing, we are familiar with that contrast which poets have drawn between the insignificance of man and the vastness of the universe of stars, and, for another, it is astronomy or cosmology which of all kinds of science attracted to itself most powerfully the attention of all thinking persons in the decade which has just closed. But in the past there seemed to go along with this realisation of man's insignificance two assumptions : first, that somehow the earth, or at least the solar system, occupied a central position in the universe ; and secondly, that man was in some sense the crowning achievement of creation. (There were also theological assumptions with which for the moment we are not concerned.) The astronomers, mathematicians and physicists of our own day have come near measuring the full extent of the universe and determining its constitutive elements ; and in terms of time and space that universe has grown so vast as to defy an imagination which has difficulty in attaching much reality—or significance—even to a period of a thousand years, and is merely stunned when the astronomer begins to deal in millions of light-years. But that in itself— this growth of the extent of the universe—is of little importance in comparison with other pronouncements of science. It has become certain that astronomically the solar system is not the centre of the universe but an insignificant cluster of bodies whirling on the edge of a far vaster system. The dream that the other heavenly bodies outside our solar system could be inhabited has gone, since life, as we understand life, must be impossible in worlds in which the very atoms cannot keep their heads. More than this, one great scientist had propounded the question whether life itself might be no more than a disease of matter in its old age. *That* was what had become of the assumption that man is creation's highest achievement. Indeed, one might not be beside the mark in asking whether in the new picture of the universe which modern science had revealed there was room for anything which could be called highest achievement. The words seem robbed of meaning in a universe capable of being represented as a gigantic clock which, once wound

up, is slowly running down and can never be wound
up again.

Turn now to quite a different field—to analytical
psychology. We have come to believe—it is reflected
in our daily talk—that the mind of man has two
realms, the conscious and the unconscious (or sub-
conscious). The conscious—the realm of what
we may loosely call self-directed endeavour—is small
in comparison with the realm of the unconscious,
whence forces of incalculable potency are for ever
striving to thrust their way into the conscious realm
with results too often disastrous to the individual's
health and happiness. Often within the realm of
the conscious these forces of the unconscious,
primeval lusts and fears, masquerade as virtues or
reasonable ideas ; but by careful analytical study
their mask is torn away. Man's inner life tends to
be viewed as a bundle of " complexes "—" systems
of connected ideas with a strong emotional tone and
a tendency to produce actions of a certain definite
character "—as they have been defined. And one
of the greatest of analytical psychologists has suggested that the Ego itself is no more than a complex.
So may we learn to-day to doubt the one thing which
it had been left us to doubt—our own identity, ourselves. It is true enough that the analytical
psychologist holds out the hope that if we accept his
views he can improve our chances of health and
happiness—but at the price of a determinist philosophy and the loss of our identity. Nor do we
find any comfort if we turn from him to the
Behaviourist, for he also is a rigid determinist, and
he will tell us that we are no more than pos-
sibilities of reaction—mere trigger-mechanisms or
penny-in-the-slot machines. If thought exists, it

is not worth troubling about, and words serve but as signals.

Now, clearly the poet can accept the doctrine that life is a disease of matter in its old age. A latter-day Baudelaire could make poetry out of that, and the old title *Fleurs du Mal* might continue to serve. Such a poetry, again, would not be much gloomier than *Ecclesiastes*. After all, there is nothing new in the thought that the universe is unfriendly to man, or at best so little interested in him that in all his aspirations and sufferings he does but disquiet himself in a vain shadow. Yet when the worst has been said and has been accepted concerning man's place in the physical universe, men we remain, and to us our concerns matter intensely. We can say and believe that, if the universe is immense and sinister, even more immense is the courage which accepts and challenges its hostility—all this on condition that on one side, at any rate, we do not form part of the physical universe. But destroy that condition, and how can any faith in himself continue in a man who is convinced that courage itself and faith itself are no more than physical reactions capable of being measured in the same kind of way as we measure, for instance, an electric potential ? Who can have courage to say he is captain of his soul if he really believes that he has no soul ?

But, we may say, is it not possible that science has fallen into error in the past ? Are yet new philosophical interpretations of the universe to be ushered in by the physicists and mathematicians ? On the extreme verge of the decade there is some justification for asking that question, since the public have had broadcast to them the doctrine that in the physical universe examined in the light of the latest mathematical research there is no justification to be found for a philosophic determinism. But to follow up this line of thought would carry us too far away from our immediate purpose.

The sole instrument of science is the analytic reason, and it has always been open to challenge the efficacy of this instrument for discovering the truth about life or for measuring the value of life. And certainly the challenge has been sounded. It was, indeed, sounded many years ago—it is an eternal challenge on the lips of all men who have seen so many disastrous consequences flowing from the analytical reasoning as that has been employed not so much by students of physical science as by statesmen, theologians and economists. For these also claim to employ the tool of analytical reason. The challenge, then, is sounded in every field of human activity, but our concern is more particularly with the field of poetic thought. And in that field the loudest and clearest challenge was uttered by the Romantic writers and critics. About their theories there will be something to be said when the third main literary tendency of the Twenties comes under consideration—the Neo-Classical Movement, which is also an Anti-Romantic Movement. The manifestation of the protest against analytic reason (or intellectualism) especially characteristic of the Nineteen-twenties is not a kind of Romanticism at all. It is not easy to label. On one side it operates as a revived interest in mysticism and in certain characteristic attitudes of the Metaphysicals of the seventeenth century. Or again, without any special or express reference to any former type of poetical thought achievement, it holds that poetry and thought have nothing to do with one another—that although a poem which contains reasoning and explanation may be a poem, the accuracy of the reasoning and the adequacy of the explanation give no measure of its value as poetry. On yet another side it strives to recover the simplicity, the freshness of outlook and the directness of childhood. For instance, one of the best known of contemporary critics says of Mr. De La Mare that " half his poems are really bred out of his perpetual recovery of childhood, when reason was in abeyance and the ' facts of life ' not apprehended, and all things in their nakedness assailed the spirit and the senses with their full beauty and mystery."

These points must be developed a little farther.

Simplicity and directness are the two outstanding characteristics of much of the poetry written in the decade. But it must not be thought that simplicity and obscurity are incompatible. Obviously, they are compatible. An Englishman may talk with the utmost simplicity about roses to an Esquimaux and will be utterly unintelligible to his hearer. So also when the mystic poet speaks of his Rosa Mystica in the simplest language most men will fail to understand him. A child speaks very simply to a grownup and is impatient because he is not understood. And this difficulty of the grown-up may come of the very fact that the child's perception is clearer and in a sense truer than his own. But now let us consider the following criticism of Blake which has appeared in a weekly review of our own time :

" His work is no latter day Talmud to which the initiate alone holds the key ; his readers should give up hope of ' interpreting ' and explaining and rest content to ' look into his pictures,' and let the cadences of his poetry saturate their minds, till their sympathies have extended from the enjoyment of obvious beauties and gradually embraced the less obvious system on which those beauties depend. A doctrine may then become clear. . . ."

Reflecting upon that, one may come to distinguish between two kinds of obscurity in poetry. The one is of the child who would be shocked and hurt if you told him he was not relying on reason : if he could find the language, he would reply that he was being perfectly reasonable, and that anyone but a blockhead would understand him. The other is the obscurity which our critic attributes to Blake—the obscurity of a man who has consciously abjured reasonableness, and who would be more annoyed than pleased if you claimed to understand him—not because he despises understanding or prides himself on being obscure, but simply because one can no more understand poetry than one can smell algebra. And in some such attitude of mind we find the origin of a great deal in modern poetry which makes *Sordello* seem like the acme of lucidity. In most cases the language itself is simple enough :

> A wall of cactus guards the virgin sound—
> Dripping through the sword-edged leaves
> The wayward milking
> Of your mental stalactites
> On the strung bells of music,
> Arrests the moment,
> Petrifies the air.

The poet, naturally, cannot abjure thought, and he need not abjure logic, but the thought and the logic are not of the essence of poetry—it is his attitude towards thought which matters. In modern criticism we find such a phrase as "the emotional apprehension of thought," and such a judgment as " In Donne . . . we find the first consciousness of felt thought." These utterances themselves will not be too clear to every reader, but perhaps it is not misleading to say that the position of mind we are now considering is one which in a proposition of Euclid admires the style without troubling itself about the correctness of the demonstration and proof. In other words, poetry and analytic reason are thought of as working in different spheres, and if these intersect they do not confuse their boundaries.

But now we advance another step in the development of this position. It might be supposed that, as poetry seen from this angle has no concern with analytic reason (with intellectualism), neither is it concerned with the truth. But the supposition would not be permitted by these poets. On the contrary, they would maintain that poetry has at command a far more potent instrument than has science for arriving at the truth, and that is intuition. Here is a characteristic proposition. " ' The Phœnix and The Turtle ' . . . is the direct embodiment through symbols which are necessarily dark, of a pure, comprehensive and self-satisfying experience, which we may call, if we please, an immediate intuition into the hidden nature of things." Shakespeare, in other words, has transcended reason. And in the essay from which the quotation is taken it is maintained that " the nature of Shakespeare's poetry is the nature of poetry." Here, indeed, we must notice an important distinction. A characteristic idea attributed to the Romantic writers is that they oppose intuition to reason—the two working as it were in complete independence. But there is another possible view of intuition which might be characteristic of the mystics—namely, that in the progress of the soul towards the ultimate truth intuition begins where reason leaves off. The poet's intuition, that quality or faculty in virtue of which he is properly called a poet, is the same as, or is related to, the vision of the mystic at prayer. The relation between the poetic and the mystic experience has been elaborated in a book which attracted much attention —*Prière et Poésie*, by the Abbé Henri Brémond, the latest exposition of the *vates sacer* theory of the poet's function—a vates who prophesies, but teaches nothing and instructs no one. Stripped of all intention to inform, to instruct, to convert, poetry becomes Pure Poetry, or Poetry for Poetry's Sake.

" Poetry for Poetry's Sake " is the title of Professor A. C. Bradley's Inaugural Lecture from the Oxford Chair of Poetry, delivered, indeed, in the opening years of this century, but representing an outlook which is manifested in much of the poetry of the Twenties. Obviously suggested by the better-known phrase, " Art for Art's sake," it is safer than that—at least it is less likely to be rejected by poets and critics in this country.[1] Adopting, then, this phrase for the moment, one may now proceed to inquire what can be deduced from it as to the technique of poetry. Obviously, in the first place, in poetry which does not inform or instruct or persuade but has for its office to produce in the reader a special kind of experience, there can be no completely valid separation of technique (i.e. form) from subject-matter (i.e. content). Technique and subject-matter will be no more than two aspects of the same thing, that will be the view of those who

[1] It has been strongly attacked by Mr. I. A. Richards in his *Principles of Literary Criticism.*

accept the doctrine of Poetry for Poetry's Sake.
Others who do not follow that banner will remark
that the poets who do not wish their poetry to be
understood, who do not analyse and syllogise, are
precisely the poets who expend the greatest amount
of labour upon the technical side of the work and are
proud to call themselves conscientious artists. To
be accused of writing *vers libre* ought to be considered by them the bitterest irony, since they have
only exchanged old shackles for newer and heavier.
This was necessary for them. For establishing
communication (one hesitates to say " for expressing
themselves ") they cannot rely upon all the same
means as their predecessors : they are confined
to the sounds of the poetry and to the associations of
the words. Quotation will best illustrate these
points. Miss Edith Sitwell is speaking of Miss
Marianne Moore's poem *Black Earth*. This poem
is about an elephant—or perhaps one should say this
is an elephant-poem—but there also comes into it
some notion of " the animal state of consciousness
shaping itself from within." Miss Sitwell comments :

" Notice how admirably her technique in this
case is fitted to the subject. It conveys the great
lumbering gait, and though the lines are short, the
huge size of the subject. And this is done by a
technical device which Miss Moore uses a thousand
times in other poems . . . the trick of ending lines
with such words as ' of,' ' and,' or ' a,' indeed, even
the trick of ending a line in the middle of the word."

Of another poem she says :

" The dissonances which end the lines in the place
of rhymes give the discontent of the subject, its

groping in the blackness, without finding what it is
groping for. May I ask you to notice the curious
effect that the alternation of the dull muted r's and
sounded r's have in this poem ? They give the
effect of the hoarse voice of an animal."

Such an attitude towards technique seems like
the natural consequence of a doctrine that poetry
exists wholly in its own right. For if a poem is
something *sui generis*, it may be assumed that it
must, like " the animal state of consciousness " in
Miss Sitwell's critique, " shape itself from within."
The only sense in which the final, shaped product
can legitimately be described as free verse, is that it
has not had its shape imposed from without.

" Means of communication " were mentioned
above, and the chief were said to be the sound of
the verse and the associations aroused by words.
Some modern poets, it is true, have attempted to find
a third in typography. Mallarmé's *Jamais un Coup
de Dés n'abolira le Hasard* has found imitators in this
country and in America. To a certain extent such
devices are pure freakishness, but in so far as new
developments in technique demand a special kind
of reading, special typographical devices may become
necessary.[1] On this point, however, there is no
time or occasion to dwell. A word or two must be
said of association. The quotations from Miss
Sitwell illustrate the extent to which certain poets
rely upon association : even more suggestive quotations might have been taken from the same writer's

[1] Of one such experiment it is written by an admirer : " Parentheses he
uses for sotto voce pronunciation ; or, if they occur in the middle of a
word, as in ' the taxi-man p(ee)ps his whistle,' they denote a certain
quality of the letters enclosed—here the actual sharp whistling sound
between the opening and closing (the two p's) of the taxi-man's lips."

book on Pope. But it is in reading the mystic poets that we are most vividly reminded how extensive a use of association was forced upon them by the very nature of their thought. If you transcend the syllogism, one might say, you must be borne upward on the wings of association. In a moment of vision I see what is ineffable in the sense that no familiar method of description will serve to communicate my experience. Here those things which to logic are contradictory and irreconcilable are merged in a higher unity. My only hope of evoking in you some part of the effect of that vision is by finding the word or group of words whose associated images and emotions will work as an evocatory charm. My words cease to have their everyday commonplace references : they become symbols. I say the words " rosa mystica " ; and that will grow up in your imagination, which is present to mine. Other words which seem to be credited with that influence by the mystics are : light, darkness, abyss, fullness, clearness. Not words only nor groups of words have this evocatory or associative power, but also and in a special degree particular rhythms and cadences. And, indeed, it is very natural that the poetry of the mystic should of all poetry approach most closely to music.

But the associative or evocatory aspect of language has been of interest not only to the mystics or to those poets like Baudelaire, who, far removed from mysticism, yet hold the doctrine that " La poésie n'a pas d'autre but qu'elle-même," but also to that type of thought which became prominent in the Twenties and might be called Neo-Classicism. It is by technique as much as by anything that this poetry is different from other classical or classicist poetry. The technique appears to have been strongly influenced by the spread of a new interest in psychology (possibly the strongest formative influence upon literature in this decade) and particularly the psychology of the unconscious, or semi-conscious mind. And the style is erudite in its allusiveness : or, if that is a wrong description, the style relies for its effect upon a certain degree (a pretty high degree) of erudition in the listener. But for the purposes of the present inquiry the most interesting characteristics of Neo-Classicism are the hostility to Romantic poetry and Romantic thought, which the name itself implies, and still more the attack upon certain kinds of scientific and philo-sophical thinking. Concerning the hostility to Romance not much need be said. The Romantics are accused of having lost touch with life and carried men's minds away into an unreal region—an un-healthy region in which disproportion and hysteria hold sway. From Romanticism we are called back to that Greek ideal of harmony, proportion, control, to a world of common sense and decorum. But perhaps the most serious accusation brought against the Romantics is that they failed in point of sensi-bility. And since sensibility had been the great merit of seventeenth-century poets such as Donne and the Metaphysicals, we find the Neo-Classics, like the believers in Pure Poetry, holding these poets up for our special admiration. " The poets of the seventeenth century . . . possessed a mechanism of sensibility which could devour any kind of experi-ence." But far more significant is the challenge to certain types of scientific thought sounded by the Neo-Classics—and sounded in the name of good stout sense and logical thinking, not in the name of the mystic's transcendent vision of the truth. Consider what Professor Babbitt has to say about psycho-analysis : " The Freudian then proceeds to develop what may be true of the hysterical degenerate into a complete view of life." Again, of the mechanistic philosophy of science he says it cannot satisfy " the true positivist " because it involves factors that are " infinite and therefore beyond calculation."

The swerve away from Romanticism takes a different form in the critical theory of Mr. I. A. Richards. That critical theory is based in great part upon psychological research, and it expressly abjures metaphysics, a type of thought which he considers as only likely to lead its followers into a wilderness where they will die of inanition. In a sense, then, he might be expected not to take much interest in those implications of pessimism which many poets and critics have developed out of the thoughts of the men of science—physicists, biologists and analytical psychologists. Starting from a purely psychological basis, he judges a poem according to its effect of helping us or of hindering us in building up the organisation of our experience—or, in other words, in raising or lowering our standard of response. In loose language, his position is that poetry must be praised or condemned according as it helps or hinders us in our conduct of life. If it were permitted still more loosely to represent this as a theory that good poetry makes for the happiness of ourselves—individual and community, we should have Mr. Richards starting out from modern psychology and Professor Irving Babbitt, who has travelled on a longer road from the Nicomachean Ethics, meeting and shaking hands.

Here, at the risk of a certain amount of repeating
or overlapping, it may be advisable to build up
what is little more than a note upon the influence of
analytical psychology on the poetry of the Twenties,
since, as has already been said, that was probably
the strongest formative influence which can be
discerned. From the nature of the case that influence has been even more powerful in fiction than
in poetry. To some extent the influence has been
direct, to some extent indirect. In its indirect action
it appears as the influence of other literatures—
notably of Russian fiction ; but the direct action is
probably more important. It was certain to operate
so soon as psychology renounced the sphygmometer
and the æsthesiometer in favour of the analytic
methods of Freud and Jung, simply because Freud
and Jung interested themselves in the growth and
development of consciousness and its relation to the
sub-conscious. For it began to occur to novelists
and poets that the obscure mechanisms of the mind
—those which hover at the threshold of full consciousness—might not only provide them with a vast
new subject-matter, but, a far more original and
daring thought, might actually be harnessed to a
literary purpose. Thus some of the new poetry
could almost be called a kind of psychological
experimentation. Something has been already said
on this point when association and evocation were
in discussion. But there is something more—there
is the spectacle of the poet eavesdropping at that
mysterious door which shuts off his conscious mind
from his sub-conscious and noting in his book the
confused and nonsensical babble that he hears from
within—catching, also, those lingering, slowly dis-
persed echoes which the consciously uttered word

awakens on the other side of the threshold. And this note on the influence of psychology may end by remarking that the new technique was made easier for those who wrote in the Nineteen-twenties by the dazzlingly original researches into assonances, dissonances, cross rhythms and so on carried out and practically applied by Gerard Manley Hopkins so long ago as the Sixties of the last century—in the days when Browning was in *The Ring and the Book* writing blank verse which shocked his hearers but might perhaps suggest to a more enlightened generation that in a dim kind of way he also was aware of new and quite different prosodies.

Our review of three main tendencies amounts shortly to this. There has been a reaction against Victorian ideals and achievements in poetry accompanied by a special kind of pessimism and disillusionment which derives at least a large part of its strength from the recent discoveries and speculations of the scientists. Poetical thought has reacted in different ways under pressure of this pessimism and disillusionment. Some have declared that poetry has nothing to do with science, ethics, metaphysics, but exists in its own right and spins its own world, as it were, out of itself. Others say that while science and philosophy work in one region and poetry in another, it is in the region of poetry, and by the means of which poetry disposes, that the ultimate truth is to be found. Yet a third group challenges science and philosophy on their own ground and, while maintaining close and intimate touch with possible realities, finds its own interpretation of these. More shortly the first group say that science is irrelevant, the second that it is unimportant, and the third that it is wrong. All have

8

strongly manifested that interest in the foundations and the beginnings of the workings of consciousness which forms the special field of psychology, and all have been influenced either in their subject-matter or in their technique or in both by the work of psychologists.

Following upon the procedure of earlier chapters, we have to consider next how Browning stands out against this background, and what the critics have had to say about him.   Or perhaps it will be more convenient to start with a general statement on that last point—what the critics have had to say about him.   They have had very little to say about him, but it is clear that they are still a little puzzled.   One calls him " exuberant and greedy " ; another says he is both admirable and insufferable ; conceited and self-assertive.   A third describes him as a robust and bustling casuist full of eager, mundane curiosity. But there is a most slender basis upon which to erect any generalisations.   In other words, the critics will not be found to give much help in linking Browning to his background in this decade.

Let us begin by repeating a point already made, that this age laughs at the Victorians and that Browning is assumed to be a characteristic Victorian. And in a day which is paying so heavy a price for the tigerish brilliance of Mr. Lytton Strachey by having to endure all his jackals, it is curious that no book has been written about Browning in what might be expected to pass for the style or treatment of *Eminent Victorians*.   Perhaps we may find the germs of Stracheyism in such stray utterances as this of Mr. Aldous Huxley—" the poetry of that infinitely respectable rebel, that profoundly Anglican wor-shipper of passion, Robert Browning."   More

Stracheyesque are references to peculiarities in the person or dress of Browning—" Noted for his unfailingly immaculate lemon-yellow gloves." And yet what a rich material lies here neglected ! By what mercy of Providence has it happened that no one has yet worked up a complete biography from it ? There are not only the lemon-yellow gloves, there is the diet of potatoes, the loud harsh voice, the habit of placing himself in disagreeable bodily proximity to the person with whom he was speaking and puffing and blowing in that person's face ; the disappointment at not being invited to the Jubilee celebrations in the Abbey ; the dinners with duchesses ; the removal from Warwick Crescent to De Vere Gardens ; the defence of Pen's paintings of the nude ; the shocked horror at George Sand's entourage—and a score of other delights. Mr. F. L. Lucas did, indeed, resuscitate an unfriendly remark —" Who is that too-exuberant financier ? "—and Mr. Shanks repeoples the old mare's nest of negro or Jewish origins. From a whole biography in the new manner we have been spared. And yet, as a matter of fact, all these things *are* significant, and an attempt will be made in later chapters to unfold their significance.

Not only Victorian, but an optimist, a man who thought that all was right with the world, blind to the misery and suffering which surrounded him on all sides. Or perhaps he was insincere in his optimism —perhaps not consciously or deliberately insincere, but deceiving himself. He shouted and banged out his optimism in an effort to drown the unpleasant truths which his inner consciousness kept whispering to him. And yet it is curious that the critics of his optimism should have been blind to certain parts of

Browning's thought.   Two examples of the blindness may be given.   The first of these is a very
obvious example—the isolating from their context of
these so often quoted lines—

> God's in His Heaven,
> All's right with the world.

That Browning was not ignorant of suffering and
misery ought to be clear enough from the rest of the
poem—or from the single episode in *Pippa* from
which the lines are taken.   They are taken from the
scene in which the main characters are Ottima and
Sebald.   Sebald has just murdered Ottima's husband, and none of the more sordid elements in the
intrigue are omitted.   Moreover, the girl who utters
the lines has hanging over her head a plot which is
to send her to Rome in order that she may there
become a prostitute—" at Rome the courtesans
perish off every three years and I can entice her
thither—have indeed begun operations already."
Once more, then, it is clear that Browning was not
blind to evil.   Whether he wrongly analysed it is
another matter.   The other example concerns perhaps an even broader issue.   Critics maintain that
Browning's creed of the immense importance of
individual man in the total scheme of things cannot
be squared with what science teaches of the cosmic
insignificance of man.   The inference seems to be
that if he had read Einstein or Jeans he would have
changed his views.   But Browning's own contemporaries were also saying that man was insignificant in comparison with the heavens.   In fact,
Hamlet, in fact, the prophets of the Old Testament,
had suspected that man was a thing of no account

The insignificance is only a question of degree, and it is not likely that Browning would have been perturbed if he had thought that humanity was merely a moment's episode in the countless drama of astronomical time.   His answer—for he did make an answer—can be opposed to scientists of this day, just as much as to the scientists of the Eighteen-seventies—and again, whether it is a complete answer, it is not here relevant to discuss.   He begins by saying that when he examined himself to discover what were the things which he could say that he knew, he found only two—his own existence (including all that he thought and felt) and the existence of something outside himself—

I have questioned and am answered.   Question, answer pre-
    suppose
Two points : that the thing itself which questions, answers,—is,
    it knows ;
As it also knows the thing perceived outside itself—a force
Actual ere its own beginning, operative through its course,
Unaffected by its end . . .
What before caused all the causes, what effect of all effects
Haply follows,—these are fancy.   Ask the rush if it suspects
Whence and how the stream that floats it had a rise, and where
    and how
Falls or flows on still !   What answer makes the rush except that
    now
Certainly it floats and is, and, no less certain than itself,
Is the everyway external stream that runs through shoal and
    shelf,
Floats it onward, leaves it—may be—wrecked at last . . .
. . . May be !   mere surmise not knowledge : much conjecture
    styled belief,
What the rush conceives the stream means through the voyage
    blind and brief.

These lines may read more like a page from a meta-physical treatise than a poem, but the point of view

cannot be confuted by remarking that it is such a
very small rush and such a very large stream—or
even that there is only one very little rush in an
illimitable stream. As a matter of fact, the thought
expressed in the passage is modern, though the poem
(*La Saisiaz*) is more than half a century old. (In
honesty it must be added that the main thought of
the whole poem could not be called modern.) And
as optimism is here in question, it is relevant to
quote a few more lines. Browning—who in this
poem is undoubtedly speaking *in propria persona*—
considers what results accrue if he is committed to
the belief that while all that he sees around him is an
illusion, his own joys and sorrows remain real :

Still,—with no more Nature, no more Man as riddle to be read.
Only my own joys and sorrows now to reckon real instead—
I must say—or choke in silence—" Howsoever came my fate,
Sorrow did and joy did nowise,—life well weighed,—preponder-
    ate."

The new experiments made by recent poets in the
technique—especially in the prosody—of poetry
brought about a great interest in the work of Gerard
Manley Hopkins, whom at least one critic of repute
has called the greatest poet of his age : and his age
was the second half of the last century. The hint
has already been given that certain features of
Browning's technique might be explained by supposing, not—as has hitherto been supposed—that
they were due to a defective sense of melody and
rhythm, but to a vague feeling about for new paths
in which Hopkins was already walking. Browning's
work on this side has been treated in a new and
sympathetic way by Professor Elton in his *Survey*,
and the points which he has made there wait to be

developed and treated more comprehensively by some critic more competent than the present writer. Still it remains true that Browning would have rejected emphatically the doctrine of Poetry for Poetry's Sake. On this aspect of his work we need not linger except to suggest that no one of his own time experimented more widely and freely than Browning, and that this in itself must have helped on the development of a new attitude in poets towards questions of technique. At the same time his failures in this matter—which cannot be denied by any serious critic—and his deliberate subordination of sound to sense would win him short shrift from any critic to-day who, fresh from Gerard Hopkins or Edith Sitwell, sat down to read *Asolando*. That does not seem to have happened.

The obscurity of Browning's poetry was a stumbling-block, even to his most favourable critics, from 1840 almost up to the present time. But in our own day those who admire Mr. Joyce, Miss Gertrude Stein, Mr. T. S. Eliot and the Sitwells can hardly condemn him on this count. They cannot object to obscurity in poetry. There is, however, in this matter a difference between Browning and the moderns. Robert Browning tried to be lucid, and was often surprised when his readers complained of his obscurity. He thought lucidity a virtue : the moderns do not. In other words, whereas Browning really did desire to be understood, many poets of the Twenties would have felt disappointed, if not insulted, if their readers claimed or even attempted to understand them. Therefore, although they cannot attribute it as a fault to Browning that he is obscure, they can say that his obscurity is of the wrong kind.

Two qualities so much prized in our own day do
not characterise very much of Browning's work,
though they are certainly not always absent. These
are directness and economy of style. It is not
unusual to hear that the day of long poems is over.
If that were true (and it is not) it would help to
explain the neglect cf Browning in certain circles.
He is long-winded and he is cumbersome in much of
his work. He uses up over a thousand lines of blank
verse in *Red Cotton Nightcap Country* before he
really gets to grips with his story. *Sordello* is nearly
as bad. Even *Christmas Eve* begins in the middle.
Like a kitten with a mouse he scampers round and
round his subject with occasional feints and rushes
towards it for a long time before he makes his final
pounce. What moderns require in a poet is the
speed and certainty of a flash of lightning. It is
not always that Browning fails in that respect.
Some of his narratives are models in story-telling,
for instance, *The Pied Piper of Hamelin* or *The
Flight of the Duchess*. And in economy of means to
an end it would be difficult to quote anything better
than *My Star*, *Porphyria's Lover*, *The Heretic'.
Tragedy* and a score at least of the lyrics of his best
period.

Nor can it be said that naïveté or a child-like
freshness of outlook prevail in his poetry. It is
rather a poetry with the outlook of a man of the
world. Perhaps there are things in *Pippa Passes*
especially in what has been put into the mouth of
Pippa herself, which exhibit something like naïveté
but even this claim might be seriously disputed. On
the other hand, two points are worth making here
though it does not fall within the scope of this study
to develop them. The first is that a great deal of

what passes for simplicity nowadays is probably in a high degree artificial. This perhaps applies even more to painting than to poetry. And, secondly, much evidence is now available for a belief that children are not so very child-like after all.

It will not be convenient in this place to inquire of the admirers of mysticism what judgment they would pass on Browning, since that is to form the subject of a later chapter. At first sight a favourable judgment could not be expected, but actually there are elements in his work which in an age that has so much to say of Donne and Crashaw and George Herbert might have been expected to attract attention if only by their incongruity with the rest of his work— especially with that part of it which tempted one critic of the Twenties to call him " a robust and bustling casuist " and another of an earlier date to say that all his poetry was summed up in the line— " *Bang, whang, whang*, goes the drum, *tootle-te-tootle* the fife."

If not a mystic, then a Romantic—that seems to be the conclusion arrived at by at least one contemporary critic. It appears to be more than ever difficult to discover what the name Romantic implies, or at least to make up all the implications into one parcel. Perhaps the characteristics of the Romantic poets to which most attention is now being given are their depreciation of the understanding (analytic reason), their belief in the sacredness of the emotions, their impatience of restraint and order, and their shrinking from the realities of life. And if these qualities do make up the essence of Romanticism, it is further assumed that they are all to be found in Browning. For instance, Dean Inge has called him a misologist, and Professor Irving Babbitt

sees in him a clear example of the poet whose
emotional values are all awry. In this critic's
judgment Browning has abjured right reason, is
flaccid in his spirituality, formless in his verse, and
does not attempt to control his emotions or observe
decorum. But so far from believing in the sacredness of the emotions or the essential good-hearted-
ness of man (as Rousseau is said to have done)
Browning believed in " The Corruption of Man's
Heart." He believed in the sacredness of only one
emotion, namely, love. And when the special
characteristics of love, as Browning understood that
word, are examined, they are found to make up
something very different from love as Shelley, for
instance, understood it. Browning's love is refined
away until it almost ceases to have any tinge of desire
in it. Love consoles us, explains life, keeps us alive
It is not the contrary or the opposite of reason, nor,
on the other hand, does its work begin where reason
leaves off. If it can be compared with intuition
then it must be with the intuition of Bergson rather
than of the mystics, since it is not a power by which
we apprehend the ultimate truth, but a power which
enables us to be in sympathy with our surroundings,
to " get inside " our world. It is distinct from
reason in the sense that a man may aim at perfecting
his reason and may at the same time eschew
love—and the whole of *Paracelsus* is a picture of
such an attempt. Paracelsus found that to eschew
love was fatal, and Sordello found that only by love
can the man of genius bring himself to acquiesce in
the limits which time and space and physical dis-
abilities in general impose upon the exercise of his
powers. In one of the not many poems in which
Browning avowedly speaks in his own person, he

cries that in the world, as God has made it—if only
we could see it—" All is beauty : and knowing this
is love," with which may be compared what Paracelsus says, " In my own heart love had not been
made wise." Gathering up these and other indica-
tions, we may suppose that, though in Browning's
mind love and reason are distinct, there is between
them a harmony, as it were, pre-ordained. The
special point which it is relevant to insist upon here
is that love, so far from being something formless or
impatient of restraint, is precisely that which imposes
a measure upon man's powers—a μέτριον. How far
such a conception is self-consistent—that is to say,
how far it is immune against the attacks of the
logician—is another question. It is enough to notice
that it is a conception only with great difficulty to be
reconciled with the attitude which Professor Irving
Babbitt, for instance, regards as an essential characteristic of the romantic imagination.

When all Browning's faults have been recounted,
his critics remember as the chief of his virtues the
acuteness of his psychological insight ; his power of
analysing motive, for instance, or, more broadly, his
keen understanding of the way in which men's minds
work. He knew how the mind of a worldly prelate
moved when he was defending himself against a
second-rate journalist ; how the mind of a spiritualist
charlatan works, the mind of a painter or bishop of
the Renaissance, of a Hellenistic poet and thinker—
of a hundred men and women of different types.
What is curious is that a generation like our own, so
interested in the psychological novel, should not
have taken note of the special character of the Browning psychology. It was Swinburne who first perceived that special character (see page 52), and we

have seen how Mr. Shaw compressed the same
criticism into an epigram. And yet Browning
created characters—the Caliban, whom Mr. Shaw
thought untrue to life, really does insist on coming to
life ; so does Bishop Blougram ; so does Fra Lippo
Lippi.   But the truth is that Browning, in spite of
all appearances, does not as a rule probe deep—not
so deep as Hardy or Proust or Dostoevsky.   Nor has
he much to say of the part played by the unconscious
in the workings of the mind. A trace may be found
here and there :

> Underneath rolls what Mind may hide, not tame,
> An element which works beyond our guess,
> Soul, the unsounded sea—whose lift of surge
> Spite of all superstition, lets emerge
> In flower and foam, Feeling from out the deeps
> Mind arrogates no mastery upon—
> Distinct indisputably.   Has there gone
> To dig up, drag forth, render smooth from rough
> Mind's flooring,—operosity enough ?
> . . . But Soul's sea,—drawn whence,
> Fed how, forced whither,—by what evidence
> Of ebb and flow, that's felt beneath the tread,
> Soul has its course 'neath Mind's work overhead,—
> Who tells of, tracks to source the founts of Soul ?
>   (*Charles Avison :* stanza vii.)

This is not precisely the philosophy of the unconscious (the whole stanza really deserves study), but it
is near enough to that to excite interest.   Elsewhere
he uses much the same language :

> I who detecting what vice underlies
> Thought's superstruction—fancy's sludge and slime.

The study of background in the third and last
of the decades selected must be completed, as in the
other decades also, by reflecting upon these quest-

ions : " Did the Nineteen-twenties praise and blame
the poet for those qualities we should expect them to
praise and blame ?   And did they notice in his work
those elements or tendencies which might have been
expected to interest them ? "   To these questions,
when asked of the two other decades, a negative
answer was given.   But of the Nineteen-twenties
we must speak differently.   In attacking Browning's
optimism and in repudiating his social and moral
code they took the attitude which they would seem
bound to take.   But it is remarkable that they should
not have felt bound, in repudiating his optimism, to
make mention at least of that passage in *Fifine* which
was quoted in the last chapter (see page 75), and in
which Browning (or rather Don Juan) says that the
more disagreeable a truth is, the more likely it is to
be true.   That is not optimism, and it is very far
removed from the Victorian attitude of mind as that
is represented to us by contemporary critics.   Again
it was to be foreseen that those who have forsaken
Shelley for Crashaw should dislike the romantic vein
in Browning, and that, generally speaking, all
enemies of romance should accuse Browning of
flaccid spirituality.   But if they had read *Sordello*
they could hardly have refrained from remarking
upon its central thought—as new as it was unromantic—that love, instead of being an emancipator,
is the very reverse, a moderator, a controlling
influence which does not help man to blind himself
to the awkward realities of existence, but reconciles
him to them.   And finally, to repeat what was said
only a few lines above, it is remarkable that an age
so taken up with psychological analysis should not
have appraised the work of Browning from that
point of view.   And since it is, above all, the psycho-

logical conflicts in the individual which interest the
mind of to-day, it is strange that no one has taken
the trouble to inquire what signs there are in Browning of such a conflict. It is precisely this inquiry
which will be attempted in the second part of the
present study.

PART II
CONFLICT

CHAPTER VI

THE OUTWARD MAN

THERE is plenty of material for anyone who wishes to form a picture of Robert Browning in his later years—and, indeed, there are still amongst us those who met and talked with him. The impressions he created upon those who met him naturally varied—and, indeed, are flatly contradictory in some cases. There are few more attractive pictures than that contained in Gosse's *Personalia* : there are few more unattractive than that presented by Mary Gladstone (Mrs. Drew) in her Diary.[1] But on certain points there is almost universal agreement—for instance, that he was genial, talkative, warm-hearted, differing from Tennyson about as widely as one man can differ from another in outward appearance, in manner and address. Tennyson, for instance, hid his shyness under a rather gruff, alarming manner (here again Mary Gladstone's Diary is worth consulting) and the unfriendly-disposed spoke of him as " always wrapped up in a cloud of mysterious self-adoration."

Browning was never averse from discussing the works of other poets, and was generous in his praise of those whom he admired. He would quote their verses at length—his memory was prodigious— and he could criticise them : and his criticisms were often acute. It is all the more curious that on the subject of his own poetry this genial and talkative

---

[1] See page 141.

man was comparatively reticent. Here again he
stands in complete contrast to Tennyson, who did
not hesitate to express admiration of his own achievements with a frankness and ingenuous simplicity
that remind one of Rodin. Browning was willing
enough to read his poetry to his friends, but most
unwilling to discuss it with them. He would neither
discuss it with friends nor, as a rule, defend it against
the attacks of hostile critics.

A little time may be devoted to an attempt to
measuring and commenting upon this reticence. If
ever a man may be forgiven for writing about his own
work, it is when in the earliest stages of his first love
affair the lady invites him to tell her all about himself. And this invitation Elizabeth Barrett issued to
Robert Browning in the very beginnings of their
correspondence. Some response he did make, but
neither then nor at any other point in their correspondence did he become eloquent or even copious
on the subject. And when the two were married,
and in their Florentine home pursued their poet's
work, neither spoke to the other of what was going
forward, until each poem or set of poems was complete and ready for the press. The most striking
example of this is the familiar story of the way in
which Elizabeth Barrett Browning handed to her
husband the manuscript of *Sonnets from the Portu-
guese*. Now, we know too much about this pair of
poets to be able to believe that their reticence came
of any distrust or lack of sympathy. On the contrary, we know that Mrs. Browning was the only
critic to whose suggestions Browning listened or
whose emendations he would receive, and there are
many who consider that she was on the whole his
best, his most discerning, critic. Another matter

may be alluded to which illustrates this trait in Browning's character. In the biography by Hall Griffin and Minchin we are told that at the very time when he was writing *The Pied Piper of Hamelin* for little Willie Macready, his father was himself engaged upon a poem on exactly the same subject. After the father had written some sixty lines, he discovered what his son was doing and abandoned the attempt. But the elder Mr. Browning made this discovery by accident—it had not been his son's intention to tell him, although the story was one which his father must have read to him many times in his boyhood, and the news that it was being turned into verse would have interested and delighted the older man. In spite of these and other facts of the same kind there are few great men known to us whom we should find it more difficult to think of as secretive.

Was this reticence due to an over-sensitiveness to criticism ? Certainly Browning had a great hatred of professional journalistic critics, whom he described as a " verminous tribe." A letter which he wrote to Alfred Domett in 1842 throws some light upon his attitude towards them : " One poor bedevilling idiot, whose performance reached me last night only, told a friend of mine the night before that, ' how *in reality* he admired beyond measure this and the other book of Mr. B's, but that *in the review*, he thought it best to, &c. &c.' This Abhorson boasted that he got £400 a year by his practices ! " And what he said of critics in *Pacchiarotto* is well enough known. But in none of these utterances is there any sign of an over-sensitiveness to criticism. He disliked and despised critics, and in another letter to Alfred Domett he strongly censures Tennyson for having altered his text to suit the comments made upon it in reviews. " The alterations are insane. *Whatever* is touched is spoiled. . . . I have been with Moxon this morning, who tells me that he is miserably thin-skinned, sensitive to criticism (foolish criticism)." The evidence appears to be conclusive that he was not contemptuous because the critics were hostile, but because they were dishonest— either directly and deliberately dishonest like the " Abhorson " of his letter to Domett or indirectly dishonest because they judged him without having read him. How far he was justified in this estimate should be clear to anyone who has read the second chapter of the present book.

He never penned any Apologia or Defence or any long explanatory Preface. He who so often showed the combative side of his nature—and he could even be pugnacious—scarcely took the trouble to defend himself. It is extraordinary that when the *Pall Mall* reprinted a poem of his from *The Century Magazine* with misprints and additions he did not write directly to the editor in order to get the matter put right : he wrote to Mrs. Frank Hill, and ended the letter thus: " So does the charge of unintelligibility attach itself to your poor friend—who can kick nobody "—and how untrue that last statement is will be clear to anyone who will recall the unhappy episode of the FitzGerald sonnet. It is, then, not easy to understand why he did not deal directly and faithfully with " the verminous tribe." Much more difficult is it to understand why he was reluctant to enlighten even his own friends—those whose opinions he is known to have valued. He did, indeed, on rare occasions explain and defend himself to these. There is a letter to Ruskin (printed in

W. G. Collingwood's *Life*, 1900 edition, pp. 163-7)
which comes nearer than anything else he ever wrote
to a detailed defence of his work—and is unknown
to most people because omitted from the better-
known biographies. It is in the main an answer to
a charge of obscurity, and is too long to be quoted
here in full, but this much is relevant : " A poet's
affair is with God,—to whom he is accountable, and
of whom is his reward ; "—and this also : " I shall
never change my point of sight, or feel other than
disconcerted and apprehensive when the public,
critics and all, begin to understand and approve me."
To other correspondents he sometimes gave an explanation of some particular point of difficulty in his
poetry. But even when all this is taken into account,
even when we have given full weight to his belief
that the poet's affair is with God, we remain puzzled,
since the poet whose affair was with God did, after
all, publish his poems.

His attitude to the Browning Society, and in particular his toleration of the ineptitudes of J. T.
Nettleship and the shortcomings of Mrs. Orr, have
already been mentioned. It is one thing to allow
your enemies to misinterpret you on the ground that
vengeance is the Almighty's, but common charity
would seem to require that you should not allow
your friends to go astray. In other words, Browning
might at least have spoken out directly to the Society,
to Nettleship and to Mrs. Orr. He was friendly
disposed to the Society. He expressed his gratitude
at the effect of their work upon the sale of his books
—that he was over generous in this does not matter.
Now, it was entirely discreet and right that he should
not allow himself to be too much mixed up with the
Society's affairs ; that, in Sir Edmund Gosse's words,

he should occupy a seat in the front row of the stalls but never consent to appear on the stage.[1] It was entirely discreet and right that he should refuse to look over the proofs of the Browning Society's papers—(" I have the appearance of authorising whatever notice it may contain, considerable or otherwise, since I receive it and say nothing—which is as good as consenting, to the ordinary apprehension "). But it was extraordinary that, for instance, although he was well acquainted with Nettleship and corresponded with him, he never protested against the paper on *Childe Roland*. Even gratitude to Nettleship cannot explain this. He never got farther than telling him in a letter that his poems were " each and all . . . purely *dramatic*, with no sort of attempt at esoteric meaning." It is still more extraordinary and even exasperating that while to a private correspondent, only a remote acquaintance, he consented to give a true and clear explanation of *Another Way of Love*, he allowed Mrs. Orr to print an explanation which robs that poem of its most characteristic dramatic climax.[2] And yet he admired Mrs. Orr's *Handbook* and sang its praises to Mary Gladstone.

Nor is it open to us to suppose that he hesitated to explain this or that particular passage for fear lest he should be drawn into the impossible attempt to put into other words that which in the poems themselves already stood expressed in the clearest language of which he had been capable. For in his long letter to Ruskin, after having asserted that in his poetry he had been as clear as his powers per-

[1] Sir Edmund Gosse informed the present writer that Browning asked him not to join the Browning Society, and did not desire that any of his friends should join it.
[2] See page 80.

mitted, he does proceed to deal with small individual points—e.g. to explain the line—

> Stand still, true poet that you are,

and to justify scanning " foldskirts " as a trochee.

There is an air of petulance about his letter to Ruskin, and Browning himself was not unaware of it. He was annoyed because Ruskin was in a certain sense coming between him and his God. That same petulance repeats itself in most, though not all, of the few letters which he wrote in explanation of difficult passages. And sometimes he gave the impression that he himself did not know the meaning of what he had written. Besides the familiar story of " Now God only knows what it means," there is this in Mr. E. F. Benson's *As We Were*—" His admirers there (Cambridge) had started a Browning Society . . . which met to discuss and elucidate the poet's more difficult moods, and he attended one of these meetings, but was said to be unable to throw any light on certain of the conundrums of his own making, which were referred to him." It is, indeed, possible that on this, as other occasions, he did actually or metaphorically shrug his shoulders and say once again that he could not find better words to express his meaning, but it is also possible that his general attitude in the matter—his reticence, his petulance, his embarrassment—is best explained by assuming that to some extent consciously, to a larger extent unconsciously, he dissociated his poetry from the rest of his life.

Let us consider what evidence can be given in support of this theory of dissociation. Some evidence can be got from the *Pacchiarotto* volume. In

the poem which gives its name to the volume he
protests against a habit of critics of importing their
own meanings into his poetry, but in the second
poem he protests against another habit of theirs—
the habit of reading him into his own poems, of
going to his poems because they are the key with
which to unlock his heart.   To them he says :

> Which of you did I enable
>   Once to slip inside my breast,
> There to catalogue and label
>   What I like least, what love best.
> Hope and fear, believe and doubt of,
>   Seek and shun, respect—deride ?
> Who has right to make a rout of
>   Rarities he found inside ?

And the same theme is repeated in *House*.   Here we
have very plainly expressed the picture of the poet's
verse as a closed domain.   Into that domain he
admits no one, to find out what he himself thinks
and feels :

> Outside should suffice for evidence.

This, indeed, is no more than the uttering in verse of
what he many times said in letters and conversations,
that his work was essentially dramatic—the utterance
of imaginary persons, and not the expression of his
own views and feelings.   But when we come to the
next poem in the series, we have a rather different
idea put forward.   That poem is *Shop*.   It is supposed
to be addressed to a dead tradesman :

> So, friend, your shop was all your house.

That is in accents of surprise.   For the speaker had
thought from the riches and curiosities he saw in

the shop window that the owner must have some
wonderful private house of his own.   It might be—

> Some suburb-palace, parked about.
>   And gated grandly, built last year :
> The four mile walk keeps off the gout ;
>   Or big seat sold by bankrupt peer :
>   But then he takes the rail, that's clear.

But that conjecture was all wrong.   The shop was
all—there was no house at all.

> Nowise !   At back of all that spread
>   Of merchandize, woe's me, I find
> A hole i' the wall where, heels by head,
>   The owner couched, his ware behind
>   —In cupboard suited to his mind.

And the speaker moralises.   This sort of life is all
wrong.   The merchant should have something else
in his life besides trafficking—

> I want to know a butcher paints,
>   A baker rhymes for his pursuit,
> Candlestick-maker much acquaints
>   His soul with song, or, haply mute,
>   Blows his brains out upon the flute !

> But—shop each day and all day long !
>   Friend, your good angel slept, your star
> Suffered eclipse, fate did you wrong !
>   From where these sorts of treasures are,
>   There should our hearts be—Christ, how far !

Is the lesson preached only to the butcher, the baker,
and the candlestick-maker ?   Or is the poet included
also ?   At first the temptation is to suppose that the
poem is a sort of sermon against a purely money-
grubbing materialism.   Pretty certainly, however,
it is more than that.   Browning gives a hint in
the Epilogue to *Men and Women* (*One Word More*).
In that poem he shows how the poet grows tired of
the business of always being poet, just as Raphael,

tired of being a painter, would write a century of
sonnets and Dante prepares to paint an angel, because no artist, whatever his art, can be contented
for all his life with just that.

> Ay, of all the artists living, loving,
> None but would forego his proper dowry,—
> Does he paint ? he fain would write a poem,—
> Does he write ? he fain would paint a picture,
> Put to proof art alien to the artist's,
> Once and only once, and for one only,
> So to be a man and leave the artist,
>   Gain the man's joy, miss the artist's sorrow.

The hint is unmistakable—the problem does exist
for Browning whether a man may not be greater than
an artist—life greater than poetry and overlapping it
on every side.   The hint is repeated elsewhere.   The
lover in *The Last Ride Together* cries to the poet :

> You hold things beautiful the best
>   And pace them in rhyme so, side by side.
> 'Tis something, nay 'tis much : but then
> Have you yourself what's best for men ?

And Norbert, the hero of *In a Balcony*, says :

> We live and they experiment on life
> These poets, painters, all who stand aloof
> To overlook the farther.

Then there is a passage in *The Two Poets of Croisic*
in which the narrator comments upon his story in
a concluding passage remarkable for its beauty and
power (stanzas clii to the end) from which this much
may be quoted :

> There's a simple test
> Would serve, when people take on them to weigh
> The works of poets, " Who was better, best,
>   This, that, the other bard ? . . . . . .
>   . . . . End the strife
> By asking, " Which one led a happy life ? "

All this evidence does not by itself prove that Browning tended to dissociate his poetry from the rest of his life, since all that it seems to amount to is the perfectly reasonable idea that no one, not even a great artist, can afford to be nothing but an artist. But when it is taken in conjunction with Browning's reticence about his poetry and with the inconsistencies in his attitude towards all his critics, it does in some degree at least corroborate the suggestion that he tended much more than most poets—and more indeed than was wholly reasonable—to shut off his poetry from the rest of his life. For it is one thing for the poet to try his hand at painting or sculpture : it is quite a different thing for a man to be a poet to-day and a sculptor to-morrow, and never or very rarely to allow the poet and the sculptor to meet.

Of this dissociation there is other evidence. We may find it if we consider the outward man, that is to say, if we recall his appearance, his manner, his method of conducting his affairs. And perhaps we might hardly do better than to begin by recalling Max Beerbohm's caricature of the poet taking tea with the Browning Society of London. The neat little smiling man in Max Beerbohm's cartoon looks like a well-to-do doctor or solicitor surrounded by a most depressing company of ill-dressed, heavily serious intellectuals. Browning was always careful in his dress, a habit most contrary to all that is expected of poets. Mrs. Bridell Fox described him in his early days as " just a trifle of a dandy, addicted to lemon-coloured gloves and such things : quite ' the glass of fashion and the mould of form.' " Less attractive but not more poetical is the description of him by Miss Arnould, who was far from

sharing her brothers' admiration. She saw in him
a pasty-faced youth of Jewish appearance with long
heavily pomaded locks : a youth over-confident in
manner and loud in speech. To return to his later
years, there is much evidence for the accuracy of
Max Beerbohm's version. Messrs. Hall Griffin
and Minchin write : " His appearance was robust,
manly and impressive ; his abundant white hair,
expressive glance and alert demeanour made him a
noticeable figure in any assemblage ; but there was
nothing in his look which distinctly proclaimed the
poet." All his portraits confirm this account of him,
and everyone will recall the famous saying, " I like
Browning : he isn't like a damned literary man."
They may be invited now to forget that other remark
about " a too exuberant financier." But the most
attractive picture of him in his later days has been
painted by Mr. E. F. Benson in *As We Were*. He
there relates how on one occasion Browning was
entertained at Newnham by some enthusiastic students. After tea his hostess, " in a frenzy of diffidence and devotion, told him that she had woven a
crown of roses for him, from which all thorns and
unpleasant moistures had been banished, and might
she have the extreme honour of placing it on his
head." The poet consented. " So there he sat,
bland and ruddy, and slightly buttery from the
muffins, with the crown of pink roses laid upon his
white locks and looking like a lamb decked for
sacrifice." Then he fulfilled his promise to read
one of his poems. His choice fell upon *A Serenade
at the Villa*, but after he had recited a line or two,
suddenly he caught sight in the mirror of " the
image of himself crowned with pink roses. He
broke into a peal of the most jovial laughter. ' My

dear young ladies,' he said, ' shall I not read *The Patriot* instead ?   It was roses, roses, all the way.' ''

One tries in vain to see Tennyson in the same situation.   The ending would have been different.

Yet not any more in his old age than in his youth did he make upon all who met him an equally happy impression by his personal appearance and outward habits.   Mary Gladstone, who met him in 1870, said: '' Mr. B. is not altogether a remarkable person to look at, and talks in a rather too self-confident way.'' It was worse still next time she met the poet in March 1874.   '' After to Mr. Baring's for music. . . . Felt dreadfully tired and done and Browning brushed my face with his beard.''   Three years later than that she had not yet conquered her repugnance.   '' He talks everybody down with his dreadful voice, and always places his person in such disagreeable proximity with yours and puffs and blows and spits in your face.   I tried to think of Abt Vogler, but it was no use—he couldn't ever have written it.''   And yet when she heard of his death she spoke of her feeling of '' ungetoverable personal loss ''—but it may be that she was thinking of Abt Vogler.

As much as in his outward appearance, Browning was unpoetical in his way of ordering his life. Jowett's comment is well known : '' I had no idea there was a perfectly sensible poet in the world,'' and his friend and benefactor Kenyon said that he was struck by his common sense and its '' contrast to his muddy metaphysical poetry.''   There was in him a touch of the '' bon bourgeois '' who loomed so large in Victor Hugo.   He exercised care in the management of his financial affairs, and hated to leave debts unpaid. He does not seem to have been in any practical matter absent-minded or careless. Many of his letters to his son and to Miss Isa Blagden are the letters one would expect from an entirely practical and unromantic British business man. In his early middle life it would seem from his wife's letters that he suffered from nervous irritability, and that in these moods his sense of proportion broke down, but there is no evidence that this continued into his later life.

Then, again, in early youth he seems to have had a quite normal healthy liking for social occasions. " I heard of you, dear Miss Barrett, between a Polka and a Cellarius the other evening." It would seem, however, as if Mrs. Browning's influence tended to extinguish this taste for a time—or, if not to extinguish his taste, to alter his attitude in these matters. During their married life he did not shun social occasions, but he did not welcome them in the same spirit as in his later years.

By way of digression it is interesting to notice that this loud-voiced, over-confident man of Mary Gladstone's painting detested public speaking. This hatred endured through his life and is said to account for his refusal to be named Lord Rector of the University of Glasgow or Lord Rector of the University of St. Andrews (in 1875 and 1877 respectively). Thirty years before this he had written to Elizabeth Barrett telling her of his anguish of mind at having to respond to the toast of Poetry at a public dinner.

It was an irony of fate that in 1846 Robert Browning should have written, " I am convinced that general society depresses my spirits more than any other cause," and that in the Seventies or Eighties people should have been saying of him that "he had dinnered himself away." For in the later part of his life—at almost any time after 1873—he had become a prominent figure in London society. He was present at all social functions. It is recorded of him that he was aggrieved because he had received no summons to be present at the Jubilee service in Westminster Abbey. He accepted invitations to the country houses of the great ; scandal said that " he was proposing to Lady Ashburton . . . at least she let it be thought so," and all the good it seems to have done him was to earn him the reputation of being a snob.

And this irony of fate takes on another aspect when we recall what this poet had written in *Paracelsus* and in *Sordello* about the world's praises and the world's pleasures :

> The scheme was realized
> Too suddenly in one respect : a crowd
> Praising, eyes quick to see, and lips as loud
> To speak, delicious homage to receive . . .
> . . . Courted thus at unawares,
> In spite of his pretensions and his cares,
> He caught himself shamefully hankering
> After the obvious petty joys that spring
> From true life, fain relinquish pedestal
> And condescend with pleasures. . . .

In this our own day, though the accusations of snobbery and of worldliness still make themselves heard, the generality of readers of Browning are little perturbed and less pained by them. They do not see in his sudden immersion into mundanities the true cause of the waning of his poetic lights, so much as an accompanying circumstance. But it may be that not even this is a correct or full interpretation of this side of the man. This side of him was at war

with another side—there is that much justification
for the apprehension felt by some of his friends and
for the malice of his ill-wishers.   The single instance
of Browning's complete good sense and unpoetic
exterior is a truly remarkable exception to the rule
which hundreds of illustrious instances have established—that poets are far from home in Belgravia;
that they are *genus irritabile*, and that they have no
love of neatness in dress.   More than this, there is a
definite danger of critics distorting the facts of the
case and misinterpreting the poet's poetry in order to
see reflected in it the worldly and even rather bourgeois element in his character.   It would be much
nearer the truth to suggest that the non-poetical
elements in his character reflected or were tempered
by some of the influences which form his poetry—
by his generosity, for instance, and his noble modesty.   Thus the view of Jowett from which one
sentence has been quoted continues to this effect—
" entirely free from enmity, jealousy, or any other
littleness, and thinking no more of himself than if he
were an ordinary man."   And Jowett was certainly
not a sentimentalist.

While it is important not to exaggerate the inconsistencies in his character to the point of suggesting
that he was positively unbalanced—a case for a
pathologist—yet there are grounds for thinking them
more important than has generally been recognised.
By calling them important, no more is meant in this
context than that the explanation of them might
give us a new idea of his poetry—present it in a new
perspective.   Let us first very briefly consider what
they amount to as far as we have gone.   There are
first the inconsistencies in the outward man—the
philosophic poet who dressed like a prosperous

solicitor and frequented the tables of the great.
Then there are the inconsistencies in his attitude
(so far as that found expression in conduct) towards
poetry in general and his own poetry in particular.
A talkative, frank, courageous man, he was not averse
from discussing other men's poetry, but he shrank
from talking about his own.[1]   And what is the explanation of all this ?   It was suggested that Browning consciously or unconsciously dissociated poetry
from the rest of his life—that he kept apart Robert
Browning the poet and Robert Browning the citizen.
But the word " dissociation " is very little more than
a summing up of the inconsistencies.   It goes very
little way towards affording an explanation : it goes
only thus far, that it has certain psychological
associations, amongst which is the association with
conflict.   Without any hazardous attempt at a
psychological analysis, we may perhaps consider
in the remainder of this study what evidences his
poetry and what is known of his life afford of any
kind of conflict in him.   We pass from inconsistencies in the outward man to inconsistencies in
his poetry.   Something may be said here by way of
anticipating what is to follow.   It will be considered
whether his moments of poetic creation—or rather,
if the term may be admitted, of poetic incubation [2]—
were not accompanied by a certain distress of mind,

[1] Oscar Browning, however, in *Memories of Sixty Years* writes:
" Browning's conversation was a great contrast to George Eliot's.   She
was always serious, always gave you of her best.   Browning rarely discussed serious topics, philosophical, literary or artistic ; his talk was that
of a man of the world."

[2] Incubation may be a more appropriate metaphor, because his distress of mind seems to have set in before the actual moment of making
poetry had arrived.   But it is not a really satisfactory term, because the
distress continued after the poem had been completed.   Whilst the
distress afflicted him, activities were unchained which, when they could
not find an outlet in verse-making, had to be discharged in sculpture, or
modelling in clay, or some such pursuit.

10

rather more intense than most poets have experienced. Once he had, as it were, expelled the poem, the after-results of this distress might well take the form of some unwillingness (conscious or unconscious) to remember [1] it or converse about it. There does not seem to have been, at any rate in the years when he was producing his greatest work, much of the atmosphere of " felicitous fulfilment of function " in his labour of creation, even though he often worked so rapidly, nor much of the craftsman's delight and self-absorption in his task. It seems to have been an effort to him to bring himself to his writing-desk, and the *Love Letters* tell us a plain story of strain and turmoil and physical reactions. In his later years—the years that followed the publication of *The Ring and The Book*—things went more smoothly, inasmuch as working hours became almost a routine of his life. In those years he grasped the torch more confidently and carried it more easily, but as a torch it had become somewhat less formidable.

---

[1] Naturally, he neither did nor could always forget. He had, for example, to revise his poems for new editions. Sometimes, however, he forgot. On one occasion a lady reported to Furnivall that Browning had failed to recognise a quotation from one of his own poems. Furnivall was filled with glee, and promptly set to work to take advantage of the situation. He arranged by correspondence that each of all the Browning Societies in this country and the United States should present the poet, on the occasion of his next birthday, which was shortly due, with a complete edition of his published poems. We are not told how the poet received this Bœotian jest.

CHAPTER VII

TIME AND ETERNITY

NEARLY all critics of Browning agree on two points : that his poetry is remarkable for its unity and self-consistency, and that he is the poet of action, and not of contemplation. There are grounds, however, upon which both criticisms can be attacked. In the first place, it is known that he entertained a profound admiration for poets of the contemplative life. A generation which finds Donne so much to its taste does not appear to realise that a century ago Browning himself was reading and loving Donne, of whom hardly anyone had heard. Nor did he lose his admiration and love. Sir Sidney Colvin, in his *Memoirs and Notes*, has written : " I recollect his (Browning's) coming out once with a long crabbedly fine screed from John Donne and declaring that he had not read or called it to mind for thirty years." Then follows a passage from the *Elegy on Mistress Boulstred*, beginning with the lines—

Spiritual treason, atheism 'tis to say
That any can thy summons disobey . . .

And again Browning himself wrote to Elizabeth Barrett that " Music should enwrap the thought as Donne says ' an amber drop enwraps a bee.' " He set to music Donne's song " Go and catch a falling star . . .," and quotes him in *The Two Poets of Croisic*, and adds, " Better and truer verse none ever wrote, than thou, revered and magisterial Donne."

In the second place, it is possible to exaggerate his interest in action. Consider, for example, the critic who writes that there is no such word as repose in Browning's vocabulary, and points out that even a description of sunrise in *Pippa* has an element of violence in it :

> O'er night's brim day boils at last :
> Boils, pure gold, o'er the cloud-cup's brim
> Where spurting and suppressed it lay. . . .

He forgets that eight lines farther down comes the line—

> Thy long blue solemn hours serenely flowing,

and also has forgotten, in another poem—

> Where the quiet-coloured end of evening smiles.

If such considerations as this should lead us to question the validity of the estimate that Browning is essentially the poet of action, and that his published work is distinguished from that of some of his contemporaries by its *unus color*, is there any crucial test which can be applied in order to decide the point? Let us take the idea of the *unus color* of his poetry. Imagine a man of keen critical discernment and mature scholarship, familiar with the whole of Browning's poetry, but wholly ignorant of the chronological order of the several poems. It would be an interesting experiment to ask him whether he could, solely upon internal evidence, arrange in their right order of date the following poems : *Humility ; A Pearl, a Girl* ; the lyric from *Ferishtah* beginning, "Not with my soul, Love . . ." ; *Mesmerism, Epilogue to Dramatis Personæ, The Twins, Tray* and *Misconceptions*. Or yet again, having informed this critic that in the 1889 edition many of the poems are out of their chronological order, we might ask him, again on the basis of internal evidence, to rearrange them in the order in which they were written. It is more than likely that the broad differences of subject and treatment between *Red Cotton Nightcap Country* and *Paracelsus* would seem suggestive. He might conclude that a certain dryness and volubility, an almost fussy buzzing round an argument or point of view in *Parleyings*, afforded evidence of a loss of power incident to old age. He might remark something like bitterness in *Dramatis Personæ* and suspect that this bitterness was not characteristic of youth—at least in a poet whose most frequent moods are so far removed from bitterness. These and similar broad differences would be discernible, but when he had exploited them to the utmost, we should expect him to conclude that they were not sufficient to dispel a belief in the essential oneness of the whole body of poems. We could not suppose that from internal evidence he would conjecture that *Johannes Agricola*[1] and *Karshish*, which are placed next to each other in the 1889 edition, are separated in time by nearly twenty years. Is there anything, again, in *Saul*, in its final shape, to suggest that the first part of it was published as a separate poem in *Dramatic Romances* ten years before the complete poem was published in *Men and Women*?

The test, if that forecast is correct, would establish the unity of Browning's poetry. But the forecast is perhaps not correct. We may hardly have done justice to our imagined critic in assuming that in the whole body of this poetry he would find nothing but at most a uniform development. On further con-

---

[1] First published in *The Monthly Repository*, 1836 (Vol. X, No. 5).

sideration we might expect him to separate out a
number of poems containing elements which, more
exactly assessed, make them seem to be out of
harmony with the rest. And it is not improbable
that he might pronounce that these incongruous
elements were important out of all proportion to
the number of poems or passages in which they
are exhibited.

In order to understand what these elements are
and to measure their importance, let us take two very
familiar poems—*Evelyn Hope* and *The Last Ride
Together*. In both the theme is apparent failure in
love. In *Evelyn Hope* a man is meditating upon his
love for a girl, much younger than himself, who has
died before he had declared himself.

> Sixteen years old when she died !
>   Perhaps she had scarcely heard my name ;
> It was not her time to love. . . .

The other lover, in *The Last Ride Together*, has
declared his love and has been rejected. But the
resemblances do not end in the fact that both men
have been apparently unsuccessful. Evelyn Hope's
lover does not think he has come too late—

> No indeed ! for God above
>   Is great to grant as mighty to make,
> And creates the love to reward the love ;
>   I claim you still for my own love's sake.

On this side of the grave he cannot claim her, but the
time will come—

> Delayed it may be for more lives yet,
>   Through worlds I shall traverse, not a few ;
> Much is to learn, much to forget
>   Ere the time be come for taking you.

Here is the conception characteristic, it is said, of Browning, and so familiar that one might almost apologise for mentioning it, of the reward delayed, of the prize more valued and more valuable because it is out of the hand's grasp. Here is a hint of the idea that if a man obtains his heart's desire in this life there is nothing left for him to strive for, because there is nothing to look forward to. Here is, finally, the idea, equally familiar perhaps, but not so frequently the subject of comment, of a soul passing through a series of existences beyond the grave. This idea first finds its expression in *Sordello* (Book VI) in a passage to which we shall return in a moment. The most familiar passage embodying it is to be found in *Old Pictures in Florence*:

> There's a fancy some lean to and others hate—
>   That when this life is ended, begins
> New work for the soul in another state,
>   Where it strives and gets weary, loses and wins.
> Where the strong and the weak, this world's congeries,
>   Repeat in large what they practised in small,
> Through life after life in unlimited series ;
>   Only the scale's to be changed, that's all.

Or perhaps in *Cristina*—

> Doubt you if, in some such moment,
>   As she fixed me, she felt clearly,
> Ages past the soul existed,
>   Here an age 'tis resting merely,
> And hence fleets again for ages. . . .

Or again in *One Word More*—

> I stand on my attainment,
> This of verse alone, one life allows me ;
> Verse and nothing else have I to give you.
> Other heights in other lives, God willing.

And in *The Last Ride Together* we have very much
the same attitude expressed in these lines :

> Who knows what's fit for us ?   Had fate
> Proposed bliss here should sublimate
> My being—had I signed the bond—
> Still one must lead some life beyond,
> Have a bliss to die with, dim-descried.

So far the resemblance between these two love poems
is fairly complete, but what has not been observed
by any commentator is that at the very end of *The
Last Ride Together* there is a complete and most
dramatic reversal of the whole of this point of view.
In order to bring this out as clearly as possible, it will
be necessary to devote some attention to the development of the thought throughout the poem.

The poem begins in a mood of the strongest resist-
ance to any idea of failure—

> My whole heart rises up to bless
> Your name in pride and thankfulness.

The lover asks, as a last boon, that once more they
may ride together, and after a moment's hesitation
that is granted, and the ride begins :

> My soul
> Smoothed itself out like a long-cramped scroll
> Freshening and fluttering in the wind. . . .

And the lover reflects, " What need to strive with a
life awry ? " which shows that for a moment he
yields to the sense of failure.   He goes on to reckon
the extent of his failure and to compare himself with
other men, since " all men strive, and who succeeds ? "   And as he passes in review the rewards of
the statesman, the soldier, the poet, the sculptor
and the musician, he finds that not one of them has

gained a boon as precious as this of his last ride with
the beloved.   Thus he asks the poet—

> Are you—poor, sick, old ere your time—
> Nearer one whit your own sublime
> Than we who never have turned a rhyme ?
>   Sing, riding's a joy !   For me, I ride.

A new courage and a new hope are growing in him,
and he reflects (this comes in the last stanza but one)
that he is only so much the better off, if his reward—
if perfect happiness, that is to say—is yet unattained.
He has yet his bliss to look forward to and to inspire
and guide him.   If he had already gained it, what
could there have been to look forward to ?   So far
we are on perfectly familiar ground—so familiar
that the reader may well ask why he has been wearied
with this repetition.   The answer is in order the
more clearly to point the contrast with the next verse,
which is quite foreign in conception to anything
which is usually associated with Browning :

> And yet—she has not spoke so long !
> What if heaven be that, fair and strong
> At life's best, with our eyes upturned
> Whither life's flower is first discerned,
>   We fixed so, ever should so abide ?
> What if we still ride on, we two,
> With life for ever old, yet new,
> Changed not in kind but in degree,
> The instant made eternity,—
> And heaven just prove that I and she
>   Ride, ride together, for ever ride ?

The idea of an endless series of existences leading
from one degree of achievement to another implies a
particular conception of the objective reality of time
succession.   Now, anyone who so thinks of time as
something possessing an objective reality cannot

attach any meaning to the phrase, " The instant made eternity." On the other hand, " The instant made eternity " enables a man within the cramped limits of however short and imperfect an existence to realise his gain, to enjoy his reward. There is a contradiction here. To put it vulgarly, you cannot have it both ways.

Before any further comment is made on this conception of the eternal moment, it will be in place to inquire whether there are many passages in Browning in which it recurs, for if *The Last Ride Together* were the only poem in which it is to be found, the matter would deserve little if any attention. It will be noticed that the idea is introduced in the last stanza of this poem in direct antithesis to the " endless series " idea contained in the last stanza but one. Exactly the same thing happens in *Old Pictures in Florence*. The stanza of that poem in which the idea of an endless series is expressed has already been quoted. It is immediately followed by this :

> Yet I hardly know. When a soul has seen
>   By means of Evil that Good is best,
>
> .   .   .   .   .
>
>   The uses of labour are surely done ;
> There remaineth a rest for the people of God :
>   And I have had troubles enough for one.

It may not be Browning who is speaking—we cannot safely assume that it is. But the passage is not easy to reconcile with the criticism that there is no such word as repose in Browning's vocabulary. Even more difficult is it to believe that *By the Fireside* is purely dramatic—that it does not reflect Browning's own feelings. Yet for the purpose of our present argument it makes no difference whether it is dram-

atic or not.   Of all that is beautiful in that poem no
lines are more beautiful than these :

> Oh moment, one and infinite !
>   The water slips o'er stock and stone ;
> The West is tender, hardly bright :
>   How gray at once is the evening grown—
> One star, its chrysolite !

But their significance has escaped notice.   No doubt
the main thought in the poem is that of the critical
moment which comes into every man's life, when he
must stake all that he has gained upon a single issue.
This is an idea generally recognised as being
characteristic of the poet.   What has not been
recognised as characteristic is the further idea that
this critical moment may in a certain sense be out of
time altogether, something which transcends time
and remains at unity with itself—" the instant made
eternity."

Next may be taken a group of passages which, considered together, seem to suggest a conception of
eternity as something enveloping, as it were, time
and space. (The conception is most difficult to
express, since the attempt to express is itself
dependent upon metaphors of time and space.)
First, in *Abt Vogler* the beautiful but fugitive invention of the composer is, as it were, taken up into
the repository of the eternal ; or, to use another
metaphor, has set upon it the seal of the eternal—

> All we have willed or hoped or dreamed of good shall exist ;
>   Not its semblance, but itself ; no beauty, nor good, nor power
> Whose voice has gone forth, but each survives for the melodist
>   When eternity affirms the conception of an hour.

(To anticipate, it is important to notice the difference between such a notion and the Platonic doctrine

of Ideas.)   Now, as eternity itself may set its seal
upon the moment within our stretch of time, so
also we from within that temporal realm may look
into eternity (may, indeed, do so at our peril : that is
a point which will be dealt with presently).   In *Dis
Aliter Visum*, the woman who is speaking blames
the man who had been her lover for not carrying
his purpose through and helping her in some—

> . . . feat, which, done, would make time break,
> And let us pent-up creatures through
> Into eternity our due. . . .

And in *A Death in the Desert*, Saint John, knowing
the weakness of understanding of his disciples, says
to them :

> . . . Ye would withdraw your sense
> From out eternity, strain it upon time. . . .

In yet another passage, much more familiar in its
thought, death is made the gateway which leads from
the temporal into the eternal :

> . . . What's death, then ?   Even now
> With so much knowledge is it hard to bear
> Brief interfusing ignorance ?   Is care
> For a creation found at fault just there—
> There where the heart breaks bond and outruns time,
> To reach, not follow, what shall be ?
> (*Gerard de Lairesse.*)

The orthodox Christian sentiment in a line of *The
Boy and the Angel*—

> With God a day endures alway—

may be compared with a far less conventional utterance in Rabbi Ben Ezra's words—

> Time's wheel runs back or stops : Potter and clay endure—

which has obvious affinities with *Abt Vogler*. A further development of the general conception of the interaction of the realms of the temporal and eternal is suggested in a line from *Charles Avison*—

> Truths escape
> Time's insufficient garniture—

as though—again employing a metaphor inadequate, if not actually misleading—portions of the eternal were embedded in the temporal. But the fullest treatment of this last aspect of the problem is to be found in Book VI of *Sordello*, in what is unfortunately, but perhaps unavoidably, one of the obscurest parts of that " wholly unintelligible " poem. The whole of this passage is so important for our immediate purpose as to deserve a somewhat detailed examination.

In the closing scene, so to speak, of the drama, Sordello is faced with the problem of accepting or rejecting the " badge," the sign of imperial authority, which his father, Taurello Salinguerra, has offered him. His troubled mind reviews his past life and his possible future. He has to decide between Palma and supreme worldly authority on the one hand, and the People and his conscience on the other. The mental effort throws an intolerable strain upon his feeble strength, and he breaks down. But in his last moments he sees clearly the secret of his failure and the possibility of his redemption—as it is not infrequent in Browning to find truth in the minds and on the lips of dying men. He becomes aware of the impact of eternity upon time. The eternal expresses or manifests itself in this sphere of time known to us, just as it may manifest itself in other spheres, taking on one shape here but quite another there—

> Once this understood,
> As suddenly he felt himself alone,
> Quite out of Time and this world . . .

He sees, moreover, that what we have just spoken of as the impact of eternity on time may be fatal unless it is controlled. Somehow the infinite must be made to fit the finite. It is in man's power—man who in a sense employs the infinite—to exercise this control. And here we may quote the actual words of the text :

> Let the employer watch the thing employed,
> Fit to the finite his infinity,
> And thus proceed for ever, in degree
> Changed but in kind the same.

" Proceed," that is, from sphere to sphere—from existence to existence. And in each sphere the infinite must be accommodated to the special circumstances (whatever they may be) of that sphere :

> A sphere is but a sphere ;
> Small, Great, are merely terms we bandy here ;
> Since to the spirit's absoluteness all
> Are like.

Here we have, apparently, placed side by side the notion of a series of existences—possibly endless, and an Absolute or Eternal Power or Soul. And so far as any attempt is made to reconcile them, it must be through the assumption that for its expression or manifestation the eternal requires the temporal.

There remain to be mentioned a group of love poems in which the notion of the supreme ecstasy of love as something transcending time is to be remarked. Taken by itself, this group might have no great significance—the idea is familiar enough, and it might even be maintained that Browning here is simply dramatic, that is to say, that he makes his lovers speak so, just because it has always been their way. But the treatment of the problem of time and eternity in the other passages with which we have been dealing may justify a reader in attaching also a special significance to a passage like this from *Eurydice* :

> Hold me but safe again within the bond
>   Of one immortal look !   All woe that was,
> Forgotten, and all terror that may be,
> Defied—no past is mine, no future : look at me !

Which is very closely akin to this :

> No past, no future—so thine arms but screen
>   The present from surprise. . . .
> > (*Ferishtah :* epilogue to *Plot Culture*.)

And to this :

> > . . . Ah Sweet—
> The moment eternal—just that and no more . . .
> > > (*Now*.)

The next quotation which it will be useful to give here is from *Luria* :

> > My own East !
> How nearer God we were !   He glows above
> With scarce an intervention, presses close
> And palpitatingly, His soul o'er ours :
> We feel Him, nor by painful reason know !
> The everlasting minute of creation
> Is felt there.
> > (*Luria*.   Act V.)

To these words Browning himself referred later on : " Time and space being purely conceptions of our own, wholly inapplicable to intelligence of another kind—with whom, as I made Luria say, there is an everlasting moment of creation, if one at all—past, present and future one and the same state."

In the view thus stated by Browning there is nothing original—indeed, it is familiar. Most churchgoers have heard it more than once from a pulpit. Yet it is important here because it is a direct statement by Browning of a belief if not in an unchanging God (the rest of the context in *Luria* is worth studying) at least a God who stands outside time and space. From this to an idealist philosophy of the Absolute seems a step which cannot be avoided, but there is clear evidence that Browning was aware of the difficulties of such a position. The clearest evidence is in one of the latest poems that he published, *Rephan*, in the *Asolando* volume. It is here that the conflict between the contemplative and the active dispositions is most vividly drawn. The picture of a static and unchanging absolute is in these lines :

> None felt distaste when better or worse
> Were uncontrastable : bless or curse
> What—in that uniform universe ?
>
> Can your world's phrase, your sense of things
> Forth-figure the Star of my God ! No springs
> No winters throughout its space. Time brings
>
> No hope, no fear ; as today shall be
> Tomorrow : advance or retreat need we
> At our standstill through eternity ?

Such was the realm of the Star Rephan. But in the midst of its perfection somehow " there lurked a seed of change that worked obscure in my heart till perfection irked." And a longing sprang up for a life of change, of difference, of perfection varied by imperfection—love by hate.

Oh, gain were indeed to see above
Supremacy ever—to move, remove,

Not reach—aspire, yet never attain
To the object aimed at !

Here, at the end of his life, the poet brings into direct conflict the two points of view—the view of reality as something timeless, and the view of it as an endless series in time. We have no right to identify his views with the views of the speaker in the poem, which he has expressly referred to in an introductory note as having been suggested by Jane Taylor's prose story *How it Strikes a Stranger.* We cannot say that to Browning the idea of an endless series of existences in which man endlessly strives towards perfection seems preferable to the idea that the reality is something independent of time and space. Indeed, we cannot even say that the speaker in that poem himself preferred such a view, since he refers to a Divine Being who holds himself separated from both the timeless, changeless realm of the Star Rephan and the imperfect and changing life of man upon earth.

The difficulties inherent in the conception of a timeless and spaceless Absolute are as old as the idealist philosophy itself, and have never yet been solved in a way which carried general conviction. If Browning arrived at some solution satisfactory to himself, it is not anywhere expressed in his poems. He was aware of the conflicting ideas, and though to one he assigned more room and weight, at least the other is present and conspicuous enough to attract more attention than it appears to have received.[1]

[1] It is only fair to say that it receives mention in Professor C. H. Herford's *Browning*, but it is only a passing mention.

11

CHAPTER VIII

MYSTICISM

BROWNING, we saw in the last chapter, is not merely inconsistent in the manner in which he talks about time and eternity, he actually contradicts himself. The contradiction is important, because it endangers what is generally looked upon as one of the essentials of his view of life—the notion that in this life we must not look to have our reward, and even more than that, that to obtain our reward in this life would be almost a disaster. One of the most characteristic instances of his self-contradiction we found in *The Last Ride Together*. There the lover who began by thinking that he must " have a bliss to die with, dim-descried," ends by believing that as a matter of fact he has already attained his bliss in an instant whose experiences transcend the boundaries of time.

The relations between the realm of time and space and the realm of the infinite and eternal, as those relations are defined or sketched in in Browning's poetry, must occupy us a little further. At the outset it may be suggested that much of Browning's thought and language on the subject suggests in some degree the thought and language of the mystics. Perhaps, then, the most convenient way in which to attack a very elusive and difficult problem will be to ask how much of the mystic there was in Browning. His commentators, with few exceptions, have described his philosophy as a kind of idealism (which obviously owes much, directly or indirectly, to Plato), and we might begin by looking at the resemblances and differences between the idealist and the mystic.

The most salient difference is that idealism is philosophical while mysticism is religious as well as philosophical. According to Miss Evelyn Underhill, an essential characteristic of the mystic is " an overwhelming consciousness of God and of his own soul " ; and his main desire is to bring his soul into contact with his God. God he conceives as an all-pervasive power at unity with itself and the particular contact with that power at which the mystic is aiming is a complete absorption of himself into God. Lastly, whereas the idealist philosopher must depend upon reasoned argument for attaining the truth about himself and God, according to the mystic reason or dialectic will not suffice to carry man within sight and hearing of his God. Direct communion with God is in moments of ecstasy in which the mystic is lifted above the temporary, the incidental, the phenomenal. In spirit he transcends the flesh. And rare and hard as those moments of vision are, so is any language difficult to find which could convey to another their nature. More than in any other intercourse the language must mean beyond itself. It must be in a special sense symbolical.

We may take these characteristics of mysticism one by one and inquire how far each is exhibited in Browning's poetry.

The " consciousness of God and of his own soul " is so constant and so assured in all that poetry, that little comment or illustration is required. Take one of the very few poems in which he expressly speaks in his own person, namely, *La Saisiaz*. There, in a moment of acute distress of mind, he examines

himself and his experience with all the earnestness
and sincerity and persistence of which he is capable,
and the conclusion of the whole long poem is that he
" at least believed in Soul, was very sure of God."
Whether it is possible to call his consciousness of
God and of his own soul overwhelming is not quite
so certain, if that implies that God and his soul stand
out in the foreground of all his thoughts and all his
writings.   It would not be true to say that he was
unintermittently preoccupied with these thoughts, in
the way in which, in their writings, the mystics were
preoccupied.   But that his consciousness amounted
to a passionate conviction which informed and lay
at the base of all his thoughts is beyond dispute.

How, in Browning's poetry, is man represented as
being brought into contact with God ?   So far as
any brief answer can be given, he is brought into
contact in two ways : by a vision or in a moment of
intensest experience (for instance, at birth or in the
break-up of the flesh in death) or by something which
in the preceding chapter was called by the rather
vague term, " the impact of the eternal and infinite."
At first sight both ways of approach look very much
like mysticism, but when they are examined more
closely, it will be seen that there are essential differences.

The vision of the full truth and glory of God or of
the spiritual world is more than the mind of man can
bear without suffering or even disaster.

> It were the seeing Him, no flesh shall dare.

From this view springs an interesting consequence.
Wordsworth in his *Intimations* Ode speaks of the
child as coming upon earth " trailing clouds of
glory," with the vision of the eternal and infinite yet

bright in him. It fades, yet not so utterly but that ever afterwards, " though inland far we be," we can still hear " the mighty waters rolling evermore." Now, there is a passage in *Bishop Blougram's Apology* which might almost seem to have been written expressly to contradict this familiar thought of Wordsworth's. The bishop, like Wordsworth, believes that in the moment of birth the child still beholds the light of the realm from which it has come—but only in a flash. And the flash leaves a wound which somehow must be healed.

> . . . the child
> Feels God a moment, ichors o'er the place. . . .

For he must be protected against the light, and will need that protection so long as he remains human. And this view of the dangerousness of the vision of God is not peculiar to Bishop Blougram : it is also put into the mouth of the Pope in *The Ring and the Book* and Saint John in *A Death in the Desert*. And in both these instances we again find something directly contrary to the suggestions of Wordsworth. It is suggested in the *Intimations* Ode that man's vision of the eternal fades as he grows older—as the shades of the prison house close in upon him. But Browning's Saint John says that advancing years " wear the thickness thin and let man see." Here are lines from the prophecy the apostle utters in his last moments :

> And how shall I assure them ? Can they have
> —They who have flesh, a veil of youth and strength
> About each spirit, that needs must bide its time,
>   Living and learning still as years assist
> Which wear the thickness thin and let man see—
> With me who hardly am withheld at all,
> But shudderingly, scarce a shred between,
> Lie bare to the universal prick of light. . . .

And so again in *The Ring and the Book* the Pope finds himself, in the " grey ultimate decrepitude " of his old age—

> Sensible of fires that more and more
> Visit a soul, in passage to the sky,
> Left nakeder than when flesh robe was new.

Again in the moment of bodily dissolution Sordello at last sees the truth :

> So seemed Sordello's closing-truth evolved
> By his flesh-half's break up.

But a far more striking instance is to be found in *Jochanan Hakkadosh*.   His last difficult words—

> Stay !
> What is . . . I would that . . . were it . . . I had been . . .
> O sudden change, as if my arid clay
> Burst into bloom !—

were confirmed by the words uttered by his " Ruach," his ghost, to his followers :

> All hail,
> Day of my soul's deliverance,—day the new
> The never-ending . . .
> Could I impart and could thy mind embrace
> The secret Tsaddik !

The sharp universal prick of light painful in this hour of death is disastrous to a man in his full manhood—a doctrine to be found in *Karshish* and in *Blougram*, of the better-known poems of Browning, and in *The Two Poets of Croisic*, of the more unfamiliar.   Karshish, wandering through Judæa, reaches Bethany, where he falls in with Lazarus, whom Christ had raised from the dead.   Lazarus in that brief time of his first death had come face to face with the full glory of the spiritual life around the earthly life. When he was brought back to earthly life, he was a changed man, so strange in his ways that he passed for a madman. His whole scale of values appeared to have been distorted.

> Heaven opened to a soul while yet on Earth,
> Earth forced on a soul's use while seeing heaven !
> The man is witless of the size, the sum,
> The value in proportion of all things,
> Or whether it be little or be much.
> Discourse to him of prodigious armaments
> Assembled to besiege his city now,
> And of the passing of a mule with gourds—
> 'Tis one ! Then take it on the other side,
> Speak of some trifling fact,—he will gaze rapt
> With stupor at its very littleness,
> (Far as I see) as if in that indeed
> He caught prodigious import, whole results. . . .

It is only with great difficulty (since his scale of values has been thus distorted) that the man can continue to guide himself through his daily life. Live on this earth he must, and so he painfully follows a clue, a thread—

> Which runs across a vast distracting orb
> Of glory on either side that meagre thread
> Which, conscious of, he must not enter yet—
> The spiritual life around this earthly life :
> The law of that is known to him as this,
> His heart and brain move there, his feet stay here.

Karshish was published in 1855. Nearly a quarter of a century later, almost precisely the same thoughts concerning man's vision of the spiritual life are expressed in *The Two Poets of Croisic*. The whole passage (stanzas lix to lxvi) is too long to be quoted in full, but the following lines give an idea of its

general import and its resemblance to the passages
from *Karshish* which have just been quoted :

lix

Well, I care, intimately care to have
    Experience how a human creature felt
In after-life who bore the burden grave
    Of certainly believing God had dealt
For once directly with him : did not rave
    —A maniac, did not find his reason melt
—An idiot, but went on, in peace or strife,
The world's way, lived an ordinary life.

lxi

Does he stand stock-like henceforth ? or proceed
    Dizzily, yet with course straightforward still,
Down-trampling vulgar hindrance ?

A little farther on he speculates by what means,
other than such experiences as befell Karshish or
René Gentilhomme, the ordinary man living his
ordinary narrow routine comes to have glimpses of
the spiritual world.   Rare though these glimpses
are, they are enough.

So do we gain enough—yet not too much
    Acquaintance with that outer element
Wherein there's operation (call it such !)
    Quite of another kind than we the pent
On earth are proper to receive.   Our hutch
    Lights up at the least chink : let roof be rent—
How inmates huddle, blinded at first spasm,
Cognizant of the sun's self through the chasm !

Finally, we may notice a curious doctrine developed
by Bishop Blougram—and not to be attributed without much risk to the poet—that the imperfections of
this life are blessed because they shield man from
too dazzling a light.

Some think Creation's meant to show Him forth :
I say it's meant to hide Him all it can,
And that's what all the blessed evil's for.

> Its use in time is to environ us,
> Our breath, our drop of dew, with shield enough
> Against that sight till we can bear its stress.
> Under a vertical sun, the exposed brain
> Less certainly would wither up at once
> Than mind confronted with the truth of Him.

Of the nature of these glimpses that light up our hutch, Browning does not have much to say in any one poem, but two things seem fairly certain : first, they are not represented as coming through those " obstinate questionings of sense," which meant so much to Wordsworth—" fallings from us, vanishings " ; secondly, they come of direct observation of our own experience and, in a way, of reasoned deductions.   The love and power which men, if they take the trouble to look, will see at work around them and within them, could not exist unless as manifestations of the Divine.

There is another way in which the individual is brought into contact with the Divine—or at least with the spiritual realm which surrounds and interpenetrates the realm of the temporal and finite. We pass, as it were, from visions to visitations, for the eternal and infinite impinges upon the finite and temporal individual.   And this impact takes place at, or rather coincides with, some intensely critical moment in the life of the individual, a crisis in the spiritual corresponding with a crisis in the temporal realm.   One might begin by pointing to what is a caricature of this idea in *Mr. Sludge the Medium*. Mr. Sludge has partly grown up into, partly thought himself into, the belief that at each moment of his life the spiritual world interferes to guide and help him :

> If I spy Charles's wain at twelve tonight,
> It warns me, " Go, nor lose another day,

And have your hair cut, Sludge ! " You laugh : and why ?
Were such a sign too hard for God to give ?
No, but Sludge seems too little for such grace.

But though this is a caricature, and though, like all
caricatures, it is an exaggeration, it is an exaggeration
of the less absurd idea found elsewhere. That the
eternal and timeless may occupy itself with the
fortunes of an individual seems ridiculous, perhaps,
to anyone who does not hold the doctrine as an
article of faith. But Browning thought the individual
immensely important. As Chesterton points out
he was constantly preoccupied with the importance
of small things. One cannot take as a caricature
these words of Sludge's :

> We find great things are made of little things,
> And little things go lessening, till at last
> Comes God behind them.   Talk of mountains now ?
> We talk of mould that heaps the mountain, mites
> That throng the mould, and God that makes the mites.
> The Name comes close behind a stomach cyst,
> The simplest of creations, just a sac
>
> .   .   .   .   .
>
> The small becomes the dreadful and immense !

A man at certain moments in his history, moments
for him of crisis, it may be, finds himself involved
in some tremendous conflux of spiritual powers ; he
becomes a centre round which forces unknown and
unreckoned by him are working out some purpose
in the eternal scheme of things. It is not always
that these confluctuating forces are, as it were,
interested in him as an individual or that they
are subserving his purposes. That is the idea not
unfamiliar in Blake—

> A robin-redbreast in a cage
> Puts all Heaven in a rage.

It is that somehow a critical moment in the individual life has synchronised or (if we must not bring in a word having associations with time) coincided with a critical moment in the history of the universe. The idea is imaged definitely enough in these lines from the *Epilogue* to *Dramatis Personæ* :

> Take the least man of all mankind, as I ;
> Look at his head and heart, find how and why
> He differs from his fellows utterly :
>
> Then, like me, watch when nature by degrees
> Grows alive round him, as in Arctic seas
> (They said of old) the instinctive water flees
>
> Toward some elected point of central rock,
> As though, for its sake only, roamed the flock
> Of waves about the waste : awhile they mock
>
> With radiance caught for the occasion,—hues
> Of blackest hell now, now such reds and blues
> As only heaven could fitly interfuse,—
>
> The mimic monarch of the whirlpool, King
> O' the current for a minute : then they wring
> Up by the roots and oversweep the thing,
>
> And hasten off to play again elsewhere
> The same part . . .

But the idea that the individual is mocked by these forces which play about him is by no means an essential part of the whole conception. Witness the too little known lyric of *Thamuris Marching* that comes towards the end of *Aristophanes' Apology* :

> Morn had the mastery as, one by one,
> All pomps produced themselves along the tract
>   .   .   .   .   .
> Thamuris marching, let no fancy slip
> Born of the fiery transport.[1] . . .
>
> Therefore the morn-ray that enriched his face,
> If it gave lambent chill, took flame again
> From flush of pride. . . .

[1] That is, the transport of nature.

What wind arrived with all the rhythms from plain,
Hill, dale, and that rough wildwood interspersed ?
Compounding these to one consummate strain,

It reached him, music ; but his own outburst
Of victory concluded the account,
And that grew song which was mere music erst.

But the most magnificent, as it is the best known,
description of this impact of the spiritual in some
instant of tense emotions and crisis is in Saul—in
the closing stanza of the poem.   David in a moment
of ecstatic rapture has foretold the supreme sacrifice
of God in Christ, and in the night he makes his way
home.

There were witnesses, cohorts about me, to left and to right,
Angels, powers, the unuttered, unseen, the alive, the aware :
I repressed, I got through them as hardly, as strugglingly there,
As a runner beset by the populace famished for news—
Life or death.   The whole earth was awakened, hell loose
    with her crews ;
And the stars of night beat with emotion, and tingled and shot
Out in fire the strong pain of pent knowledge : but I fainted
    not,
For the Hand still impelled me at once and supported, sup-
    pressed
All the tumult, and quenched it with quiet, and holy behest
Till the rapture was shut in itself, and the earth sank to rest.

But the whole stanza will recall itself to every reader
of poetry.

In quieter tones, in a less tense emotional atmosphere, the same process re-enacts itself in *By the
Fireside*.   When the lover after a moment of hesitation has spoken out all his heart to his mistress—

A moment after, and hands unseen
    Were hanging the night around us fast ;
But we knew that a bar was broken between
    Life and life : we were mixed at last
In spite of the mental screen.

The forests had done it ; there they stood ;
　We caught for a moment the powers at play :
They had mingled us so, for once and good,
　Their work was done—we might go or stay,
They relapsed to their ancient mood.

How the world is made for each of us !
　How all we perceive and know in it
Tends to some moment's product thus,
　When a soul declares itself . . .

Here, then, we have the further idea—and a most
important idea—that such a moment is, if not an
indefeasible right of the individual, at any rate part
of the reason of the existence of each individual and
that this is true of all down to the humblest.　Thus
again we read, in *Fifine*, this utterance of Don Juan
to Elvire.

Partake my confidence !　No creature's made so mean
But that, some way, it boasts, could we investigate,
Its supreme worth : fulfils, by ordinance of fate,
Its momentary task, gets glory all its own,
Tastes triumph in the world, pre-eminent, alone.
Where is the single grain of sand, mid millions heaped
Confusedly on the beach, but, did we know, has leaped
Or will leap, would we wait, i' the century, some once,
To the very throne of things ?—earth's brightest for the nonce,
When sunshine shall impinge on just that grain's facette
Which fronts him fullest, first, returns his ray with jet
Of promptest praise, thanks God best in creation's name !
(Stanza xxix.)

" Thanks God best in creation's name," coming in
this poem of 1872, recalls *The Boy and the Angel*,
which was first published in 1844 :

Morning, evening, noon and night,
" Praise God ! " sang Theocrite.

But the boy grows up and leaves his work and his
song of praise :

God said in Heaven, " Nor day nor night
Now brings the voice of my delight."

And at the words the archangel Gabriel sinks to earth and takes the boy's place and sings once more the song of praise :

> God said, " A praise is in Mine ear ;
> There is no doubt in it, no fear :
>
> So sing old worlds, and so
> New worlds that from My footstool go.
>
> Clearer loves sound other ways :
> I miss My little human praise."

Whereupon Gabriel, leaving the cell, seeks out Theocrite in Rome and finds him there dressed in his papal robes.   Gabriel calls him back once more to his cell, for weak and uncertain as the boy's song had seemed, God had missed it :

> Thy voice's praise seemed weak ; it dropped—
> Creation's chorus stopped !

No allusion has yet been made to the part played in mysticism by logic or to the language of the mystic writers.   Two points are worth developing here : first, that the mystic does not believe in the power of reason or dialectic to carry a man within sight and hearing of his God ; and secondly the language in which the mystic conveys his typical experience of communion with the Divine must be in a special sense symbolic.

The mystics are not committed to arguing that reason or logic is useless and contemptible.   In their view the individual can and must use reason to bring him as far as it can upon his way.   Now, Browning has been accused by Dean Inge of being a misologist.   How far that is just, we need not be at pains to inquire.   This much certainly is true, that—as he makes abundantly clear in *La Saisiaz*—

he does not believe that by the sole use of reason he
can arrive at any certain truth about man's destiny
in the hereafter. But if we recall a saying of the
mystic Boehme (with whose writings Browning was
undoubtedly acquainted), that " Love in its height is
as high as God," we may see at least a mystical
tendency in some lines from *Pauline* :

> How should this earth's life prove my only sphere ?
> Can I so narrow sense but that in life
> Soul still exceeds it ?   In their elements
> My soul outsoars my reason . . . .
>   . . . then what were love, set free,
> Which with the object it demands would pass
> Reason companioning the seraphim ?

With which may be compared those closing lines of
Ferishtah's Fancies which have so often puzzled
readers [1] :

> Only, at heart's utmost joy and triumph, terror
>   Sudden turns the blood to ice : a chill wind disencharms
> All the late enchantment !   What if all be error—
>   If the halo irised round my head were, Love, thine arms ?

There is, in Browning, much virtue in a dash.

There are a fair number of lines in Browning
which in point of language recall mystical poetry.
It is true that the rapt, contemplative mood is not
frequent in him, but it is not absent, and its relative
infrequency may make it all the more significant.
The line—

> Thy long blue solemn hours serenely flowing—

has already been quoted and many others included
in the preceding chapters may be recalled at this
point.   There are yet others to which allusion may

[1] The verse is judiciously omitted from *Gaudeamus* (and before that
from the *Balliol Song Book*), where the rest of the Epilogue appears set to
music by John Farmer.

be made here. Although not many poems can be said to remain contemplative throughout, there are two at least of which that can be said—*The Guardian Angel at Fano* and *Pictor Ignotus*. And perhaps the fourth stanza of the former poem is especially interesting in the present context :

> If this was ever granted, I would rest
>   My head beneath thine, while thy healing hands
> Close covered both my eyes beside thy breast,
>   Pressing the brain which too much thought expands,
> Back to its proper size again, and smoothing
> Distortion down till every nerve had soothing
>   And all lay quiet, happy and suppressed.

The quietness of *Pictor Ignotus* seems in some ways akin to the " common greyness " which silvers everything, in *Andrea del Sarto*, and Browning's masterful treatment of low lights shows itself also in—

> And now one after one seeks its lodging as star follows star
> Into eve and the blue far above us,—so blue and so far !
> (Saul.)

And this evening scene from *Fifine* :

> How quickly night comes !   Lo, already 'tis the land
> Turns sea-like ; overcrept by grey, the plains expand,
> Assume significance ; while ocean dwindles, shrinks
> Into a pettier bound : its plash and plaint, methinks,
> Six steps away, how both retire, as if their part
> Were played, another force were free to prove her art,
> Protagonist in turn !

And, far better known and better loved, the opening lines of *Love Among the Ruins* :

> Where the quiet-coloured end of evening smiles
>   Miles on miles
> On the solitary pastures where our sheep
>   Half asleep
> Tinkle homeward through the twilight, stray or stop
>   As they crop. . . .

But these passages are by themselves evidence of little more than the occasional presence of calm moods in the general heat and turmoil of his poetry. They have nothing in them particularly suggestive of mystical thought. We must then look farther afield. And perhaps the following quotation is worth examining :

> When the singers lift up their voice,
>   And the trumpets made endeavour,
> Sounding, " In God rejoice ! "
>   Saying, " In Him rejoice
> Whose mercy endureth for ever ! "
>
> Then the Temple filled with a cloud,
>   Even the House of the Lord ;
> Porch bent and pillar bowed :
>   For the presence of the Lord,
> In the glory of His cloud,
>   Had filled the House of the Lord
>   (*Epilogue to Dramatis Personæ.*)

First, the movement of these lines is unlike anything that the present writer can recall in all the wide range of rhythms that Browning employed. The movement is slow without being heavy : it is strongly controlled but full of evident power. There is control and there is exaltation. More important still, there is a hint not only of the movement but of the language which we associate with mystic writings, and not only of the language but of the kind of visionary experience. That language and that kind of vision recur in a more familiar passage :

> Proves she as the paved work of a sapphire
> Seen by Moses when he climbed the mountain ?
> Moses, Aaron, Nadab and Abihu
> Climbed and saw the very God, the Highest,
> Stand upon the paved work of a sapphire.
> Like the bodied heaven in his clearness

12

Shone the stone, the sapphire of that paved work,
When they ate and drank and saw God also !
(*One Word More*.)

The influence of the Bible is strong here both on the subject-matter, so to speak, and the language. It has already been noticed that the language of a mystic has to mean beyond itself, has to become symbolical. Symbolism of this kind—not necessarily such as we associate with the Bible—we also find in other places in Browning.

Only they see not God, I know,
Nor all that chivalry of His,
The soldier saints who, row on row,

Burn upward, each to his point of bliss . . . .

Or again :

Look not thou down but up !
To uses of the cup,
The festal board, lamp's flash and trumpet's peal,
The new wine's foaming flow,
The Master's lips a-glow !
Thou, heaven's consummate cup, what need'st thou with earth's wheel ?

And this from Sordello :

then cast
Inferior idols off their borrowed crown
Before a coming glory.   Up and down
Runs arrowy fire, while earthly forms combine
To throb the secret forth ; a touch divine—
And the scaled eyeball owns the mystic rod ;
Visibly through the garden walketh God.

To which the reader will no doubt be able to add others from *Paracelsus*, from *A Death in the Desert*, from the Pope's speech in *The Ring and the Book* and from *Christmas Eve* and *Easter Day*.

And now let us ask ourselves how much of all this is genuine mysticism. The idea of the splendour of the vision of God is familiar enough in mystical literature, but the suggestion that its very splendour may be destructive is not dwelt upon. On the other hand, it is part of the mystic way of thought to maintain that the individual must educate himself, train himself to receive the truth and pass from stage to stage of enlightenment. In the earlier stages (and few can travel beyond these in their earthly life) he will have no more than glimpses. This agrees well enough with Browning's picture of the relations between man and the eternal. The affinity between Browning and the mystics is rather less close on another side. While both agree in looking upon man's bodily limitations as a veil which prevents him from seeing the truth, they differ in this that many of the mystics proceed to argue that asceticism is necessary, otherwise the flesh will continue to be an impediment. In Browning there is no hint of an ascetic code of life except in *Easter Eve* : and we have Elizabeth Barrett Browning's authority for refusing to accept that poem as Browning's confession of faith.

We may next ask how far the notion of an impact of the eternal and infinite upon the temporal and finite agrees with mysticism. First, it must be recalled that the mystic conceives of God as an all-pervasive power, and that he aims at a complete absorption of himself into the Divine. From what has been quoted from Browning it will be clear that he too thinks of God (the eternal and the infinite) as pervading all. That one line " The spiritual life around the earthly life " suggests as much. And then again, a convulsion in the realm

of the spiritual could not produce effects within the
experience of the limited and temporal individual
unless these two realms were interlocked, unless
they interpenetrated one another. And yet, on the
whole (that is, in most passages which seem relevant),
Browning's two realms, however much they inter-
lock, seem to be able to keep themselves distinct.
Lazarus has to live his life on earth and has painfully and uncertainly to adapt himself to its rules.
There has been no practical use, as we might say,
of his vision of God. And this would seem to be
very far removed from the idea of the mystics, who
would argue that knowledge of the truth of God
must transform but will not distort—indeed, will
perfect—life on earth. For mysticism claims to be
above all things practical. Again, in the turmoil of
spirit which is a part of the impact of the infinite—
when the working out of the destiny of an individual
holds the centre of the cosmic stage—the individual
stands out distinct. Browning could not, or would
not, at any point abandon his individualism. The
nearest approach to any different sort of view is
found in the love-poems and in certain passages of
Fifine, in which the individual needs another
individual to complete his existence. But even here
there is no hint that the individuality of either is
merged. The most definitely characteristic view of
the individual in Browning is that which looks
upon him as being necessary to reflect the glory of
the Divine. Man stands upon his pin-point of
space and confronts his God. Nowhere can be
found a passage which speaks of the absorption of
man into God—not even in *La Saisiaz* where the
one point at issue is the question whether the
individual can survive bodily death.

This chapter hăs been taken up with a study of the mystical ideas in Browning, because that discussion seemed to afford a convenient framework within which to exhibit an element in his work wholly out of harmony with that set of ideas and emotions which has generally been supposed to constitute his outlook on life—his belief, that is, in a prolonged striving and a reward deferred. That is supposed to be a central idea in Browning. The strife is prolonged to a point beyond the grave, and the reward beyond that point again, and this succession may be endless. It is true that this is a central idea or doctrine, but how can such a view of man's life and man's aims be harmonised with those other views of his which have been exhibited in this and the preceding chapter, and which can, in a sense, be summed up in this, that in each individual's life there arrives one and one only culminating point—a culminating point, just as much, in the whole scheme of things ? It is in that moment, if at all, that the individual attains or fulfils ; but he lived before it and will go on living after it. What, then, becomes of the endless succession of strife, of the reward endlessly deferred ? This moment of crisis—this instant made eternity—cannot go on repeating itself endlessly in one existence after another. If it did, it would cease to be critical.

Two more remarks must be made at the end of this chapter. The disposition to see in Browning something at least of the mood of the contemplative or mystic may not be at all in the tradition of Browning criticism. Yet not every critic of distinction has consented to pronounce him the poet of action. " We might make ourselves spiritual by detaching ourselves from action and become perfect by the rejection of energy. It has often seemed to me that

Browning felt something of this." The writer is Oscar Wilde. And then again, though we cannot demand from any poet, not even a philosophic poet like Browning, complete consistency or a rigidly determined system of beliefs, yet in the points which have come under review here there is manifestly an incongruity which goes far beyond what we are accustomed to find in the least philosophical of poets, a root contradiction as surprising and as significant as if we were to find embedded in the middle of Hardy's work, translated into the words and rhythms of Hardy, *Prospice* or the *Epilogue to Asolando*.

CHAPTER IX

THE WHITE LIGHT

BROWNING'S attitude towards those who pretended to discover in his poems a key to his personal feelings and thoughts is described at some length, but in rather obscure language, by Mrs. Orr in her biography.[1] It seems to come to this, that he resented the attempt to read him into his poems as impertinent or irrelevant. But his protest did not, and, in the nature of things, could not, carry much weight with his critics either in his own lifetime or later. Furnivall spoke with violence of Browning's habit of hiding himself behind his characters, "whose necks," said he, "I for one should like to wring." In our own day two critics have made comments on this dramatisation. One of them describes the dramatis personæ as the poet's own fancy-dress ball ; the other speaks of his masquerade. The problem has not been very fully discussed by his critics, and a further examination of it will yield some curious results.

Certain things which Browning himself said about his own poetry in his letters to Elizabeth Barrett appear to have been neglected by those of his biographers and critics whose works appeared after 1898, the date of the publication of the *Love Letters*. In her first letter to Robert Browning, Elizabeth Barrett had invited him to criticise her poetry and had expressed her admiration of his

---

[1] Page 309 of the revised edition, 1908.

work. To this he replies (in what was only his second letter to her):

" Your poetry must be, cannot but be, infinitely more to me than mine to you—for you *do* what I always wanted, hoped to do, and seem only now likely to do for the first time. You speak out, *you*,—I only make men and women speak—give you truth broken into prismatic hues, and fear the pure white light, even if it is in me, but I am going to try."

And he fears that since now he must learn to do without the company of the men and women of his creation, he will find it bleak work, " this talking to the wind (for I have begun)." To this she replies : " I have been guilty of wishing that you would give the public a poem unassociated directly or indirectly with the stage, for a trial on the popular heart. I reverence the drama, but——" Then he tells her she knows nothing of him yet. " Is it true," she answers, " that I know so ' little ' of you ? And is it true, as others say, that the productions of an artist do not partake of his real nature. . . . ? It is *not* true to my mind." Browning will not accept this. " What I have printed gives no knowledge of me. . . . I have never begun, even, what I hope I was born to begin and end—' R. B.—a poem.' "

He is going to " try to speak out "—to give out the " pure white light." Indeed, he has already begun the new attempt—the attempt to produce something non-dramatic. This is all in the letters of January and February 1845. What of Browning's work was at that time in hand ? *Luria* and *A Soul's Tragedy*— both dramas. He cannot be referring to either of them. Was something in hand then which has never reached the light of day ?

Whatever the answer to that question, the important fact is that Browning had determined, apparently, before he had begun his correspondence with Elizabeth Barrett, to launch out into a new kind of poetry. Now, it might be argued that in the first ardours of love—when the contacts are being made and two souls are burning to take each other's measure—it is absurd to attach too much importance to the actual words said. These are not times when the lover sees either himself or his mistress in the right perspective. " You do not know me," cries the lover—for what lover has not ? " I am a more mysterious being than you think me." There are two answers to this argument. First, it is by no means certain that Browning was at this stage in love with Elizabeth Barrett, whom he had never seen. Secondly, even if one admits that the scene was set and the lights turned on for that romantic affair, which was already in anticipation upsetting the rhythms of the poets' souls, yet allusions to this coming change—or rather to this intended change in Browning's work—keep on recurring in the correspondence long past the point at which the unconscious tendency of a lover to make himself mysterious in the eyes of the beloved is passed. It is more than a year after the first interchange of letters, it is in April of 1846, after the last of the *Bells and Pomegranates* had been published, that there occurs in one of Browning's letters this most significant passage. In it Browning is explaining that he looks upon *Luria* and *The Soul's Tragedy* as failures. They have failed, because his heart had not been in the writing of them. And how had that come about ? It had come about through his meeting her : this had seemed to him like a deliverance from prison,

from his old ways of conceiving and writing, and had
revealed to him a new and greater way. How could
he, seeing this promise of a better kind of poetry,
take interest in the final stages of producing poems
which belonged to the old and limited kind ?

" If I had not known you *so far* THESE works
[i.e. *Luria* and *The Soul's Tragedy*] might have been
the better—as assuredly, the greater works, I trust
will follow—they would have suffered in proportion.
If you take a man from prison and set him free . . .
do you not probably cause a signal interruption to
his previously all ingrossing occupation, and sole
labour of love, of carving bone-boxes, making chains
of cherry stones, and other such time-beguiling
operations—does he ever take up that business with
the old alacrity ? No ! But he begins ploughing,
building—(castles he makes, no bone-boxes now)."

To repeat, from February 1845 to May 1846, allusions to this change that is to be in his poetry are
scattered up and down the letters. It is not once or
twice, but seven times, that Browning announces the
rising of a quite different day, the promise of a
poetry in which he will begin to express himself,
" R. B.—a poem." Elizabeth Barrett seems to sum
it all up in a letter which carries the date 26th May,
1846 :

" Several times you have hinted to me that I made
you careless for the drama, and it has puzzled me to
fancy how it could be, when I understand myself so
clearly the difficulty and the glory of dramatic art.
Yet I am conscious of wishing you to take the other
crown besides—and after having made your own
creatures speak in clear human voices, to speak
yourself out of that personality which God made,

and with the voice which he tuned into such power and sweetness of speech."

But what did the dawn bring ? What comes next after *Luria* and *The Soul's Tragedy* ? Nothing until, in 1850, *Christmas Eve* and *Easter Day*. Are these what the *Love Letters* foreshadow ? At first sight there is some reason to think that this may be so. Neither poem appears to be an attempt to present a character. The speakers in them do not live in our imaginations as do Fra Lippo Lippi or even the narrator in *The Flight of the Duchess*, and there is nothing in the title to suggest a dramatic intention in either poem. But beyond this and far more important than this there is fairly strong evidence that at least *Christmas Eve*—the earlier written of the two—is based upon an interchange of ideas which we find in the *Love Letters*. It does not appear to have been remarked that the nucleus of Christmas Eve is contained in one of Elizabeth Barrett's letters (15th August, 1846) :

" I felt unwilling, for my own part, to put on any of the liveries of the sects. The truth, as God sees it, must be something so different from these opinions about truth. . . . I believe in what is divine and floats at highest, in all these different theologies—and because the really Divine draws together souls, and tends so to a unity, I could pray anywhere and with all sorts of worshippers, from the Sistine chapel to Mr. Fox's, those kneeling and those standing. Wherever you go, in all religious societies, there is a little to revolt, and a good deal to bear with—but it is not otherwise in the world without ; and, *within*, you are especially reminded that God has to be more patient than yourself after all. Still you go quickest there, where your sympathies are least ruffled and disturbed—and I like, beyond comparison best, the simplicity of the dissenters . . . the unwritten prayer . . . the sacraments administered quickly and without charlatanism ! and the principle of a church as they hold it, *I* hold it too. . . . Well, there is enough to dissent from among the dissenters . . . you feel moreover bigotry and ignorance pressing on you on all sides, till you gasp for breath like one strangled."

There is hardly a phrase in this which could not be paralleled by some phrase in *Christmas Eve*. Browning's reply to this must also be noted :

" Dearest, I know your very meaning in what you said of religion, and responded to it with my whole soul—what you express now is for us both . . . those are my own feelings, my convictions beside—instinct confirmed by reason. Look at that injunction to ' love God with all the heart and soul and strength '—and then imagine yourself bidding any faculty, that arises towards the love of him, be still ! If in a meeting house, with the blank white walls, and a simple doctrinal exposition—all the senses should turn (from where they lie neglected) to all that sunshine in the Sistine with its music and painting, which would lift them at once to Heaven,—why should you not go forth ?—to return just as quickly, when they are nourished into a luxuriance that extinguishes, what is called, Reason's pale wavering light, lamp or whatever it is—for I have got into a confusion with thinking of our convolvuluses that climb and tangle round the rose-trees—which might be lamps or tapers ! "

Let it be considered that Browning had come to believe that this change in his poetic work, determined upon and even begun (in an experimental way perhaps) before he met Elizabeth Barrett, was now closely bound up with their joint lives ; that *she* was to help and confirm and encourage him in this new way. The new way was the way of self-expression. And here in this particular question of religious ritual there were convictions which they shared in common—Browning says so himself. Moreover, they are convictions upon matters which both he and she considered to be of the profoundest significance and weightiest moment. What more natural, then—indeed, what more inevitable—than that such convictions should form the theme of the first of the poems in the new style ?

These arguments seem difficult to controvert. Let us ask what arguments there are on the other side. There is Browning's own declaration, repeated over and over again after his wife's death, that *all* his work is dramatic except a few of the later poems. That he could have forgotten *Christmas Eve* is impossible : that he made a mental exception of it seems equally impossible—no motive could be imagined for such an attitude. There is also Mrs. Browning's statement about *Easter Day* : "I have complained of the *asceticism* in the second part, but he said it was ' one side of the question.' Don't think he has taken to the cilix—indeed, he has not—but it is his way to *see* things as passionately as other people *feel* them. . . ." If, then, *Easter Day* is not the expression of Browning's feeling, it is difficult to think that *Christmas Eve* so entirely differed from it in character, especially as the second poem is explicitly linked up with the first. Lastly, although the passages quoted from the Love Letters are certainly the nucleus of *Christmas Eve*, there is one most important difference. Elizabeth Barrett declares (and we must remember that

Browning said he wholly and entirely shared he
views): "I felt unwilling to put on any of the
liveries of the sects." Browning, in his answer
protests against the view—which is the view of the
dissenters, one presumes, in the little chapel in
Christmas Eve—that *any* faculty that arises toward
the love of God should be repressed. On the othe
hand, the speaker in *Christmas Eve*, having seen the
dissenting chapel and been repelled by all that i
ignorant and crude in that ritual, having also in a
vision seen the Christmas Eve Mass in Saint Peter'
and been present at the Göttingen professor'
lecture, finds that he must make his choice—that he
cannot stay indefinitely outside the enclosure o
some doctrine, that he must put on the livery of some
sect. Therefore he chooses the dissenters' chapel :

> Meantime, in the still recurring fear
>   Lest myself, at unawares, be found,
>   While attacking the choice of my neighbours round,
> With none of my own made—I choose here.

Now, we know from the biographies and from
Browning's own letters that, in fact, Browning did
not make a choice, that he never put on the livery
of any sect. So far did he go in this way, that the
question was for long disputed whether he was
an orthodox Christian—or a Christian in any per-
missible sense of the word.

The speculation may be indulged in, whether
Browning, when he began to write *Christmas Eve*, had
every intention of speaking out, but that something
more powerful than that intention interfered and
prevented the purpose being achieved, so that in the
end these two poems represent not his own convictions but three points of view—with one of which

we now know, he was more in sympathy than with the other two. Evidently, it will be of the first importance to inquire what was this something which frustrated his serious and often avowed intention. The inquiry is not easy, and it is only undertaken because it is germane to the main purpose of the present chapter, which is to exhibit in Browning's work the nature and results of a certain conflict.

A point, the significance of which will be developed later on, may here be accorded particular notice— and that is the confusion of thought in which Browning became involved in working out the simile of Reason's pale wavering light, convolvuluses, rose-trees, lamps and tapers.

Perhaps the best way in which to attack our present problem will be to recall the poems in which Browning did avowedly speak in the first person. Applying, then, the strictest tests, we find that there is only one such poem, *La Saisiaz*, which it will be worth while examining. Of the others, *One Word More* is admittedly a poem standing apart and not to be judged as characteristic ; and the two poems in the *Pacchiarotto* volume, in which he is speaking in person, merely amount to the statement that his poems are not keys with which to unlock his heart. Incidentally, it is of interest that *La Saisiaz* bears a date only two years later than the warning issued in *Pacchiarotto*. Of *La Saisiaz* it may first be remarked that no one nowadays reads it for its own sake. The narrative and more purely descriptive part of it deserve, perhaps, more attention than they are likely to receive now or hereafter. Browning winds his way into his theme more rapidly and certainly than in many of his later poems. The whole thing moves easily enough up to the point at which he begins to attack his central problem, the evidence of personal survival of bodily death.

Life thus owned unhappy, is there supplemental happiness
Possible and probable in life to come ? or must we count
Life a curse and not a blessing, summed up in its whole amount
Help and hindrance, joy and sorrow ?
                              Why should I want courage here ?
I will ask and have an answer—with no favour, with no fear,—
From myself.

But from that point the course of the argument is terribly involved and difficult to a degree not exceeded in any other poem of Browning's except, perhaps, *Sordello*. The very core of the whole argumentation of the poem—the paragraph beginning

What though fancy scarce may grapple with the complex and immense
—" His own world for every mortal " . . .—

will only yield its secret after not one but many most careful readings. And the difficulties are not due to vague or obscure historical allusions, but to the wavering thread of thoughts carried precariously through labyrinthine parentheses and through thickets of qualifying clauses. And to what shrine does this clue lead us ? To what white light which we may be glad to exchange for the " prismatic hues " of his dramatic poems ? To no white light at all, and to no hue which has not been discernible in those other poems. Nearly all the main thoughts are to be found in other poems—in *Mr. Sludge the Medium*, in *Saul*, *A Death in the Desert*, *Easter Day*, *The Pope*, *Fifine at the Fair* and *Francis Furini*. All that is left peculiar to this poem is the special insistence on the idea that we can hope, and no

more than hope, for a future existence, and that to
be certain of it would be in our present state no
help to us, but a hindrance.   If for " hope "
we substitute " faith," even this idea is not so
different from certain things put into the mouths
of Browning's characters such as Bishop Blougram
or the speaker, whoever he may be, in *Pisgah Sights*.

What, then, does *La Saisiaz* seem to tell us ?   Not,
it may be urged, that Browning himself *never* knew
when he was writing dramatically and when he was
not.   Nor does it prove that Browning had no
personal convictions or ideas of his own—that there
was no " white light " in him.   Indeed, it can hardly
he held to give us any help in answering the question
what it was that prevented him from writing " R.B.
—a poem."   It does, however, suggest that when
Browning attempted the non-dramatic, it took him
no farther than the dramatic.   *La Saisiaz*, as we
said above, reflects the prismatic hues of many of
the dramatic poems, but in no sense does it combine
them into a white light.   If it had done so, then, in
spite of its obscurity, it would be one of the best
known and, if not most read, then at least most
quoted of his poems.

In what way, then, are we precluded from infer-
ring that there was no white light in Browning ?   If
it was there, why could he not unveil it for us ?
" White light " is a useful metaphor of Browning's
own invention.[1]   He contrasts it with the prismatic
hues of his own dramatic poetry—" I only make
men and women speak—give you truth broken into
prismatic hues."   This can only mean that the
white light is the absolute truth or the whole of

---

[1] It is, indeed, not impossible that he was thinking of Shelley's phrase
" the white radiance of eternity."

13

truth, and that again is something which, as a philosopher would say, unifies, or co-ordinates, or is a synthesis of, our whole experience. But Browning was not first and foremost a philosopher—it is important to keep that fact well in view at this point. The philosopher in his pursuit of truth employs a dialectic—an analytic logic ; his labour is ratiocination. The poet relies on intuition and on visions. He leaps or flies across the abyss while the philosopher is laboriously laying the foundations of a bridge. Or, to use a different metaphor, he has heaven opened to him in a vision. How far he succeeds in making us also see that vision depends upon two things—the adequacy of his medium and the distinctness and clarity of his own seeing eye. And so far as Browning has in any instance or in any degree failed, it has been usual to attribute failure to the inadequacy of his medium—that is, of human language. It is not impossible, however, that he did not always manage to see very clearly what it was he desired to convey. And that may have been, as he himself hints, because he could not endure to face the central incandescence of that revealment. Certainly he desired to see, and to make others see, the world irradiated with that light —the light that shone within himself. Because it shone within himself, therefore, to impart the light would be to express himself—it would be to achieve the work for which he hoped and believed he was born—" R.B.—a poem." But it was never written.

Let us notice that though the poem was never written, the unity never achieved, the white light never transferred in full radiance to his page, that is not to say that Browning had no hint at all of what the poem might be if it ever should come to be writen. The metaphor of prismatic hues breaks down at this point, therefore, since from them alone no one could gather any hint at all of the whiteness of white light. The metaphor being abandoned, we are committed, if we are to proceed with this inquiry, to nothing less formidable than a study of the psychology of the poetic act. Adequately conducted, it would extend far beyond the limits of the present book. Even narrowed down to the strictest limits compatible with any measurable result, it remains most difficult, and happens to be one in which we have very little evidence from which to work. The poets, who alone could give evidence, have been reticent. They are not, as a rule, given to an examination of their own states of mind in moments of creation. However, it so happens that Browning himself in his Preface to the spurious *Letters of Shelley*, published in 1851, has given us a hint. From his own poems (improbable as it may seem at first sight) we can deduce something, and lastly we have something in Wordsworth and in Keats which should be of use.

What Browning has to say in the Preface does very little more than confirm what was said just now— that the poet apprehends his truth in a vision. The subjective poet, says Browning, struggles towards " Not what man sees, but what God sees—the *Ideas* of Plato, seeds of creation lying burningly on the Divine Hand. . . . Not with the combination of humanity in action, but with the primal elements of humanity he has to do ; and he digs where he stands, —preferring to seek them in his own soul as the nearest reflex of that absolute Mind, according to the intuitions of which he desires to perceive and speak." The predominating metaphors here are

of vision and light. From Wordsworth, who more
than any other of the great poets was interested in
the becoming of his poems, we may quote this from
The Prelude (Book I) :

> The Poet, gentle creature as he is,
> Hath, like the Lover, his unruly times ;
> His fits when he is neither sick nor well,
> Though no distress be near him but his own
> Unmanageable thoughts : his mind best pleased,
> While she as duteous as the mother dove
> Sits brooding, lives not always to that end,
> But like the innocent bird, hath goadings on
> That drive her as in trouble through the groves . . .
>
> .   .   .   .   .
>
> When, as becomes a man who would prepare
> For such an arduous work, I through myself
> Make rigorous inquisition, the report
> Is often cheering ; for I neither seem
> To lack that first great gift, the vital soul,
> Nor general Truths. . . .

The point there which calls for particular notice is
the fit of restlessness which comes over the poe
from time to time—a goading on (what in fashion
able jargon would now be called " an urge ") to
wards some unknown goal. However well trained
for his flight Wordsworth might think himself, ye
when it came to choosing a theme, all went awry
For if he chose a historic theme, that might b
merely because he mistook—

> Proud spring-tide swellings for a regular sea,

or yet again :

> Sometimes it suits me better to invent
> Some variegated story, in the main
> Lofty, but the unsubstantial structure melts
> Before the very sun that brightens it,
> Mist into air dissolving. Then a wish,
> My last and favourite aspiration, mounts

With yearning towards some philosophic song
Of truth that cherishes our daily life

.   .   .   .   .

But from this awful burthen I full soon
Take refuge and beguile myself with trust
That mellower years will bring a riper mind
And clearer insight.   Thus my days are past
In contradiction . . .
Humility and modest awe themselves
Betray me, serving often for a cloak
To a mere subtle selfishness ; that now
Locks every function up in blank reserve,
Now dupes me, trusting to an anxious eye
That with intrusive restlessness beats off
Simplicity and self presented truth.

Besides restlessness, there is something else that
hampers the poet. He must come to his act of
creative contemplation in a mood of complete
humility, simplicity, sincerity. He must, in short,
make an act of entire self-surrender. It might be a
mystic who had written those lines.

In the letters of Keats we find passages that
corroborate Wordsworth's account of the poetic
experience. With Wordsworth's remark about intrusive restlessness compare the following passage
from Colvin's *Keats* :

" In *Endymion* Keats had impeded and confused
his narrative by working into it much incident and
imagery symbolic of the cogitations and aspirations,
the upliftings and misgivings of his own unripe
spirit. Three years later, writing to Shelley from
his sickbed, he contrasts the former state of his
mind with his present state, saying that it was then
like a scattered pack of cards but is now sorted to a
pip."

And Keats knew well the " unruly times " of the
poet—" After working day by day at writing, I have

a swimming in my head, and feel all the effects of a mental debauch, lowness of spirits, anxiety to go on, without the power to do so." Finally, he also believed that the poet must be passive and must make a complete surrender of himself—" It struck me what quality went to form a man of achievement, especially in literature. . . . I mean *Negative Capability*, that is, when a man is capable of being in uncertainties, mysteries, doubts, without any irritable reaching after fact and reason." And again : " Let us not go hurrying about and collecting honey, bee-like buzzing here and there for knowledge of what is to be arrived at ; but let us open our leaves like a flower and be passive and receptive." Finally, just these words : " The poetical character has no self—it is everything and nothing."

We know that Browning, like Wordsworth and Keats, had his " unruly times . . . his fits when he was neither sick nor well," and that he felt those goadings on that drove him " as in trouble through the groves." Elizabeth Barrett Browning writes in one of her letters :

" Robert waits for an inclination, works by fits and starts—he can't do otherwise he says. Then reading hurts him. . . . The consequence of which is that he wants occupation and that active occupation is salvation to him with his irritable nerves, saves him from ruminating bitter cud, and from the process which I call beating his dear head against the wall till it is bruised, simply because he sees a fly there, magnified by his own two eyes almost indefinitely into some Saurian monster."

And so she was glad when he took to clay modelling and to sculpture. We know from Mrs. Orr that his

nervous excitability was such that, when he called
upon a friend, he often wondered whether he would
be able to make his way into the drawing-room.
Perhaps here we may find a special significance in
these lines from *The Guardian Angel* already quoted :

> If this was ever granted, I would rest
>   My head beneath thine, while thy healing hands
> Close-covered both my eyes beside thy breast,
>   Pressing the brain, which too much thought expands,
> Back to its proper size again, and smoothing
> Distortion down till every nerve had soothing,
>   And all lay quiet, happy and suppressed.
>
> How soon all worldly wrong would be repaired !
>   I think how I should view the earth and skies
> And sea, when once again my brow was bared
>   After thy healing, with such different eyes.

Incidentally, this is one of the few earlier poems in
which Browning is speaking avowedly for himself.

Turmoil and restlessness are very clearly pictured
here, in those interludes, at least, between the actual
times of poetic creation. But in those times themselves Browning seems to have found himself beset
with even greater difficulties than Wordsworth.
For difficult as was the entry into the viewless realm
of poesy, once there he still found himself a prey to
his own intrusive emotions. He feared the white
light. At this point we may fitly recall certain
passages in his poetry, already quoted in previous
chapters, in which he dwells upon the danger to
mortal man of having his human sight exposed to
this light. Those passages occur, it will be remembered, in *Bishop Blougram's Apology*, *A Death
in the Desert* and *Karshish*, and because the idea is
put into the mouths of three individuals so widely
different as the worldly Roman prelate, Saint John

the Divine and an Arabian medical student, it may
legitimately be ascribed to Browning himself. Certainly his attempts to confront the white light were
accompanied by great distress of mind, and there is
a special set of associations not grasped by all
readers in the beginning of the Invocation of the
first part of *The Ring and the Book*:

> Boldest of hearts that ever braved the sun
> Took sanctuary within the holier blue
> And sang a kindred soul out to his face. . . .[1]

In *Paracelsus* and in *Sordello* we find allusions to
the psychology of the poetic act. Aprile, the poet in
Paracelsus, has failed because he did not learn to
temper love with wisdom. He says:

> I could not curb
> My yearnings to possess at once the full
> Enjoyment, but neglected all the means
> Of realizing even the frailest joy.

And his own endeavour in poetry he sums up in
these words:

> Last, having thus revealed all I could love,
> Having received all love bestowed on it,
> I would die: preserving so throughout my course
> God full on me as I was full on men.

He could not bring himself to understand in time
that the task being so great and the time so brief, he
could only accomplish a part of his aim. But for

---

[1] It may not be fanciful to hold that we have here a clue to the meaning
of a much-disputed passage in this same Invocation. The poet calls
upon his Lyric Love to bless in his work.

> Some whiteness which, I judge, thy face makes proud,
> Some wanness where, I think, thy foot may fall.

Is it conceivable that the whiteness and the wanness are traces in his
own poetry of that white radiance which he praised in hers?

ur present purpose it is even more important to
notice the restlessness and bedazzlement which
possessed him in his moments of poetic vision :

> Dazzled by shapes that filled its lengths with light,
> Shapes clustered there to rule thee, not obey,
> That will not wait thy summons, will not rise
> Singly, nor when thy practised eye and hand
> Can well transfer their loveliness, but crowd
> By thee for ever, bright to thy despair ? . . .

It may be argued that Aprile is a dramatic creation,
and that we have no right to assume that Browning
is picturing his own state of mind.   That Aprile is
to some extent a dramatic creation need not be
disputed, but that there were common features in
his experience and in Browning's is demonstrable.
Compare the first of the three quotations above
with this passage from a letter to Elizabeth Barrett—
' But this is very foolish . . . and is part of an
older—indeed primitive body of mine, which I shall
never get rid of, of desiring to do nothing when I
cannot do all, seeing nothing, getting, enjoying
nothing, when there is no seeing and getting and
enjoying *wholly*." [1]   Moreover, there is a strong
probability that a poet—especially a poet of twenty-
three—in describing the psychology of another poet,
whether a real poet or a figment of his own imagination, will to some extent consciously and to a greater
extent unconsciously draw upon his own experiences.
   In Sordello we have another poet who desired to
get and enjoy everything at once, and who was, in
a sense, the victim of his own imagination.   And
since the poem to which he gave his name is to yield

[1] Compare this passage from Keats's *Letters* : " Coleridge would let go
fine isolated verisimilitude caught from the Penetralium of mystery,
from being incapable of remaining content with half-knowledge."

much material for what follows—that is to say, fo
the remaining part of our inquiry into the poeti
psychology of Browning—it is necessary to conside
in this case also how far the poem is autobiographica
and how far truly dramatic. What have Sordell
and his creator in common ? We have alread
mentioned the desire to get and to enjoy everythin
all at once. Next there is this, that just as i
Sordello the spirit was allowed with its infinite powe
to work destructively upon the weak and limite
flesh, so we know from the *Love Letters* how eve
in his early manhood Browning suffered in hi
physical constitution from the effects of high nervou
tension and the excitability and restlessness of th
poet's creative act. Again, in *Sordello* Browning wa
making a huge effort to work out a new style—
almost a new poetic language. Of this there i
complete evidence in the biographies. The poe
Sordello had this aim also among others, and th
passage in which the aim is set out contains som
of the soundest criticism ever made by a poet. No
only is the criticism worth reading on that account
but also because it is a presage, in 1840, of certai
doctrines which in this day critics and poets regar
as characteristically modern. The new languag
which Sordello tried to create failed—

> Because perceptions whole, like that he sought
> To clothe, reject so pure a work of thought
> As language : thought may take perception's place
> But hardly co-exist in any case,
> Being its mere presentment—of the whole
> By parts, the simultaneous and the sole
> By the successive and the many. Lacks
> The crowd perception ? [1] painfully it tacks

[1] As this passage in its latter part has been found obscure by som
readers, a " construe " may be justified. " The crowd painfully tack
together the thoughts into which Sordello had torn perception—he ha

> Thought to thought, which Sordello, needing such,
> Has rent perception into : it's to clutch
> And reconstruct—his office to diffuse,
> Destroy . . .

Elsewhere in the poem, in a curious passage in which, so to speak, Browning himself peeps out from behind the mask he is wearing, we have evidence that Sordello's conception of the function of poetry in its final or most perfect development is also Browning's conception. In this development the poet becomes " Dramatist, or, so to call him, Analyst " (to quote the heading of page 419 in Vol. III of the 1863 edition) :

> " Once more I cast external things away,
> And natures composite so decompose
> That . . . Why, he writes *Sordello* ! "

The inverted commas enclose Sordello's words— the rest is Browning's comment.

Other evidence of community of thought and experience between Browning and Sordello may be found in the fact that Sordello has ascribed to him many thoughts ascribed also to others of Browning's creations, which may for that reason be considered as characteristic of their creator. More valid is the identity of Sordello's thoughts with thoughts expressed in *La Saisiaz*, since in the latter poem Browning is avowedly speaking *in propria persona*. We may therefore set side by side this passage from *Sordello* (Sordello himself is speaking)—

> Forget
> Vain ordinances, I have an appeal—
> I feel, am what I feel, know what I feel ;
> So much is truth to me—

been forced to do this in order to communicate the perception. The perception has to be clutched and reconstructed—that is the work of the crowd : Sordello's work is to diffuse and destroy the perception (by the mere act of communicating it)."

in which we have an expression in the briefest possible form of that subjective idealism which Professor Henry Jones recognised as the characteristic Browning metaphysic, with these lines from *La Saisiaz* :

I have questioned and am answered. Question, answer pre-
    suppose
Two points : that the thing itself which questions, answers,—is,
    it knows ;

     •   •   •   •   •

Knowledge stands on my experience : all outside its narrow hem,
Free surmise may sport and welcome !   Pleasures, pains affect
    mankind
Just as they affect myself ?   Why, here's my neighbour, colour
    blind,
Eyes like mine to all appearance : " Green as grass " do I affirm ?
" Red as grass " he contradicts me : which employs the proper
    term ?

From such evidence of community of thought between Sordello and Aprile and Browning on this and that specific point, we may guess at a wider range of community of experience—including all those ideas and emotions which in their case accompanied or constituted the poetic act.

Let us once more consider what were the special characteristics of this experience. The first feature to be noted was a certain restlessness which arose from an unsatisfied desire to seize and to enjoy at once all forms of beauty revealed to the poet. Neither Aprile nor Sordello is a being half-angel and half-bird that fronts the sun and sings a kindred soul out to his face. They are more like moths that dash at the light and dash away in contracting or expanding spirals until their wings are singed and they die—desiring the white light and yet terrified by it. In Sordello the idea of the disruptive power of spirit forcing itself on the too-weak flesh is cardinal to the whole poem. And here it is not impossible that we have given to us, in a different metaphor, the same idea which Paracelsus embodies of the poet baffled and finally ruined in his attempt to possess the whole of beauty at once. That similarity in the conceptions can be exhibited in the following way. There is obviously a sense in which we may talk of spirit and the beauty in which spirit manifests itself as one and the same thing. In that case it is probably immaterial whether we speak of the poet's destruction being caused by the spirit trying to force itself in all the extent of its power and beauty and in one moment upon the inadequate and limited human being, or of that human being with all the inadequacies and limitations of the world of time and space in which he has his existence attempting in one moment or act to achieve and hold all beauty and power.

Aprile could not restrain himself from this vain and self-destructive aim any more than the moth can restrain itself from flying into the candle. Sordello, indeed, when it was too late, learnt the lesson of restraint, the means of sacrificing some part of the ineffable vision of power and bliss. Only love can reconcile the poet to this act of restraint and sacrifice. That is the love of humanity which Shelley—the strongest influence in Browning's time of adolescence—had made a leading theme in his poetry. We know from Browning's letters and from his biographers that to help, strengthen and comfort humanity was considered by him to be the poet's highest aim or office. He must not and cannot remain in the far region of incommunicable dreams of bliss. To help on his fellows he must be able to communicate, and if beauty in its entirety

and power is not to be communicated, he must
content himself with revealing only some part of it,
with lifting just a corner of the curtain.   And the
method which Browning chose was the method of
revealing so much of this spectacle of power and
beauty as could be seen at work in the minds of a
character or set of characters—in their minds or
their imaginary utterances.

That, then, might be one explanation of the adop-
tion of the dramatic style or treatment—that it is a
deliberate self-limitation or sacrifice by the poet.
But there is another explanation towards which most
of the preceding discussion of the problem in this
chapter will seem to have been leading, that fear or,
short of fear, trouble, turmoil, confusion may have
deterred the poet from facing the light—the central
and informing influence in his poetic vision.   And
without any attempt to derogate from Browning's
motives, we may remark that when he is discussing
with Elizabeth Barrett his plans for the future, his
intention of speaking out, and the causes which have
led him to make his work dramatic, he does not speak
of a deliberate self-limitation, and he announces his
intention of following her example and allowing the
white light to shine out.   It was not love of humanity
which had hitherto caused him to veil that light—
or it was only at times and in part that his motive
had been this.

Let us once again for a moment divest the discussion of the metaphors of light.   We have already
suggested that, interpreted in the language of logic,
this seeing of the white light of ultimate truth
amounts to a co-ordination, a harmonisation of the
poet's experience—it is the attainment of that unity
which the mystic assigns as the essential character of

he Supreme Being. It was this co-ordination or
nification of his experience, not, indeed, by means
f the logician's dialectic but by means of the poet's
ntuition or vision, which seemed so difficult a task to
Browning. Every movement which he made in this
lirection seemed to be inhibited. He stumbled and
ripped. The effects show themselves in his style.
Ie knew that *Sordello* was obscure, and he attempted
o re-write it. The attempt failed, and he consoled
imself by reflecting that while it was easy enough
o express certain things or facts, such as " bricks
nd mortar," the ideas of Sordello came near trans-
ending the powers of language. It might be laid
lown as a general rule that the obscurity of Browning
s in proportion to the earnestness of his attempt to
chieve, by intuition, a synthesis of his most intimate
houghts—as in the concluding parts of *Fifine at the
Fair*, in *La Saisiaz*, in *Easter Day*, in *Jochanan
Hakkadosh*, in *Francis Furini* and so forth. Poems
ike *Pacchiarotto* are difficult for a different reason—
namely, that Browning is deliberately indulging in
reaks of language. And Aprile and Sordello may to
his extent, if no further, be projections of their
creator's own self, that as in their case, so in his,
strenuous concentration of the mind upon the
ultimate problems of life had a definitely harmful
effect upon the physical constitution.

But all this is not to deny that he had his moments,
hough not frequent, in which the scattered and
conflicting elements of experience were co-ordinated
and unified—moments, if we prefer the language, of
vision. They are to be found in *Saul*, in *Rabbi Ben
Ezra*, in *Abt Vogler*, in *The Last Ride Together*.
Passages from his poetry have already been quoted in
he two preceding chapters which sufficiently illus-

trate this achievement. In the main, however, h
found himself bound to accept as a condition of hi
work a certain dissipation of his experience. To re
turn to his own metaphors, he had to take light no
from its source but as reflected and refracted from
this object or that. He consoled himself with th
knowledge,

> Yet my poor spark had for its source the sun,

even though it was rarely that he could direct upo
that source " the great looks which compel ligh
from its fount."

So far, in considering the psychology of th
poetic act as exhibited in Browning, we have bee
concerned with showing that certain inhibitions wer
at work here. The question inevitably arises at thi
point—" What were these inhibitions ? " The wor
"inhibition" at once suggests some theory of the kind
put forward by psycho-analysts. And it seems tha
such theories have already been brought to bear upo
Browning, inasmuch as someone has suggested tha
By the Fireside shows upon analysis clearest evidenc
that Browning was jealous of the success of his wife'
poetry and hated her for it ! One can also imagin
that *Sordello* might be taken as a proof that Brownin
suffered from an inferiority complex.[1] Such method

---

[1] To those—and they must be very few—who are at all familiar wit
Sordello, the following parallel may be interesting. Browning describe
Sordello as puny and stunted in person and prematurely aged. His lif
is wasted away in dreams of unattainable perfections. He is convince
of his own greatness in everything in which a man can be great and cal
upon his fellow-men to recognise and do honour to this supremacy. I
Dr. Bernard Hart's *Psychology of Insanity* the following passages occu
Referring to a patient in a lunatic asylum, " a man of between thirty an
forty years of age, of exceptional intelligence," he says: " It will b
remembered that he was stunted and unattractive, his muscles atrophie
and weak. . . ." During an attack of delirium the patient suffere
from the delusion that " He was immensely strong and a gymnast of th
first rank. . . . He was the greatest singer in the world, and a pro
digious orator " (*The Psychology of Insanity*, by Bernard Hart, M.D
Dr. Hart is actually quoting from Jung's *Der Inhalt der Psychose*).

f dealing with the problem raised in this chapter
1ust be left to others. To the question—of what
ature was the inhibition from which Browning
1ffered, no satisfactory answer can be suggested
y the present writer. He will travel thus far with
1e psycho-analysts as to say that there were powerful
1rces at work in the man which never succeeded
1 finding their appropriate outlet. And it is also
ot impossible that *Sordello* affords evidence that
:rowning was so far ahead of his age as to have come
ithin a hair's breadth of this modern way of stating
is own trouble. The idea of the spirit, timeless and
ut of space, destroying the poet's limited and tem-
oral bodily constitution in an attempt to express
self comes extraordinarily close to the more modern
1ea of primitive instincts and desires thrusting them-
elves into the conscious life of a man and ruining
im, body and mind. But the similarity must not
e exaggerated. Browning's " soul " eternal and free
; a very different notion from the modern " libido."

The time has come for summing up the argument
hich has run through these last four chapters. The
ttempt has been made to suggest that certain incon-
istencies and anomalies in Browning result from
deep-seated conflict in his mind. The warring
lements could be described as either the poet and
he bourgeois, or as the mystic and the poet of action.
The poet of action works within the realms of time
nd space, since these are necessary conditions of
ction. For him, action has value in itself ; and
ince attainment is the death of action, he likes to
hink of attainment as perpetually deferred. Again,
1e believes in the value of the individual and the
oncrete, the creatures of time and space. Nothing
hat can happen to the individual soul is alien to

14

him—he is full of "eager mundane curiosity." Ove
against him stands the contemplative poet whos
thought wings itself beyond the realms of time an
space, who can see each minute sealed with th
mark of the infinite and eternal because the infinit
and eternal include and swallow up the finite an
the temporal.   In his eyes nothing that has happene
of good or beautiful can perish, because it is store
up for ever in the repository of the eternal.   Th
assurance he has from God, revealed not by th
unaided reason but in a moment of direct com
munication, since "God has a few of us whom h
whispers in the ear."   The mood and the languag
are not restless and vari-coloured, but quiet and con
templative—not inert, but tense.

But the contemplative appears more rarely tha
the poet of action.   The reason seems to be tha
when Browning tried to rise above the realm o
action into the realm of contemplation, the effor
produced in him a turmoil and distress of a particula
kind.   The contemplative was eager to rise to thos
regions of vision, but the poet of action pulled hin
back.   Or, to try a different picture, Brownin
figures like a child in a fairy story who has bee
promised that he shall be allowed to enter paradis
on this one condition, that he will suppress hi
curiosity and his desires and quietly watch all tha
passes before him.   Any movement on his part wil
blur and finally destroy that paradisiacal prospec
But, try as he may, he cannot suppress himsel
The light of that supreme vision hurts his eyes-
all the beautiful things he sees stir an irresistibl
desire to clutch and possess : he springs forward t
grasp them—and the charm is broken—he find
himself back on earth again among his men an

women. The white light which shone for a brief instant is quenched.

In his earlier years this feeling of conflict and distress which accompanied the poetic act produced definite physical repercussions—a physical restlessness, headaches, neuralgia—which he tried to cure by vigorous exercise. In later life the conflict may have become less severe—through what causes cannot exactly be known. The shock of his wife's death might be expected to produce violent reactions. However this may be, after the finishing of *The Ring and the Book* there grew up a sort of dullness and dryness at the very core of his poetry. Another effect of the conflict would be a tendency to shut off his poetry from the rest of his life. In some measure, though probably not in great measure, there may have been a reluctance to admit strangers into a workshop which he had never quite succeeded in ordering properly. What he said himself was that his poetry was an affair between him and his God, not meaning thereby that it was a matter too sacred and intimate to be divulged to the curious vulgar, but that no one could help him in it any more than it is given to any man to save his neighbour's soul. But his account of the situation may be incomplete, and it may have been that he unconsciously shrank from reviving the restlessness and turmoil of the poetic moment.

The dissociation of his poetry would also tend to make him in outward life, as he mixed with his fellows, more a man of the world, more, even, of the bourgeois. It was difficult for Mary Gladstone to see in the Browning to whom she was introduced the author of *Abt Vogler*. We know it was difficult for Archbishop Benson too, for he writes in his diary for

3rd May, 1884 : " R. Browning introduced himself to me because I had quoted him in my speech. He looks strangely to me if he does really live his poems."

It is probable that he came nearer to a reconciliation of the two sides of his nature during his married life than at any other time : and this also is the period of his greatest work. His wife fostered in him the belief that he could rise above limited and partial expressions of the truth to a steady and embracing view of the whole of truth. But to such a point he never, in fact, did rise. Every now and again he caught a glimpse of that Promised Land, but it is hardly too much to say that he died upon Pisgah. Here may be found the true reason why he cannot be classed with the very greatest of poets—with the Wordsworth of the *Immortality* Ode and *Tintern Abbey* and with the Keats of the *Odes* and the *Sonnets*. But that short of the very greatest names he is yet great—and greater than most of us take him for—that would not be very difficult to establish, even if in the process it became necessary (as it pretty certainly would) to discard large masses of that work to which nothing except a kind of excited restlessness was always driving him. And it will be necessary for anyone who might desire to do him better justice than he has yet received not to blame him for the mistakes and short-sightedness of his previous critics—mid-Victorian, late-Victorian or late-Georgian. It is not likely that any critic of to-day or to-morrow will have to struggle against the tendency to condemn him as a subverter of morals. Nor yet shall we ever again come to think of him as a mighty champion of established doctrines standing between us and ruin, though perhaps we shall recognise in the man himself, when times are propitious for such a view, a courage, nobility and constancy, a generosity and power of sympathy too rare in this present day. We may come to think of him as a poet who struggled bravely to gain an insight into the hidden soul of things—fought his way towards a light that by turns eluded and blinded him. And, meanwhile, what a world he created may some day be again revealed even to the most intelligent of us—its colour, its abundance of life, its palpitating vigour, its movement that goes glorying in its own rapidity and strength. When we look below outward things in that world, we may come to see some of our own troubles and pleasures, our own most modern doubts and certainties, faithfully mirrored or forecast with a marvellous accuracy.

INDEX (I)

A. E., 43, 45
A Rebours, 43
Æsthetes.   *See*   Decadent
    Æsthetes.
Anti-Romantic Movement, 94,
    102, 109, 121–123, 125
Arnold, Matthew, 17, 19, 22, 24,
    28, 32, 35, 72
Arnould, Miss, 139
"Art for Art's Sake," 39
As we Were, 135, 140
Ashburton, Lady, 143
Athenæum, the, 25, 66, 67
Aurora Leigh, 23

Babbitt, Irving, 111, 121, 123
Bagehot, Walter, 16
Balliol Song Book, The, 175 *n.*
Baudelaire, 42, 50, 51, 55, 101,
    109
Beerbohm, Max, 35, 139
Behaviourist Psychology, 100
Benson, Archbishop E. W., 211
Benson, E. F., 135, 140
Berdoe, Dr., 70, 81
Bergson, 122
Blagden, Isa, 142
Blake, William, 103, 104, 170
Boehme, Jacob, 175
Bradley, A. C., 106
Brémond, Abbé Henri, 106
Bridell Fox, Mrs., 139
Brimley, George, 21
Brooke, Stopford, 16
Browning, Elizabeth Barrett, 23,
    32 *n.*, 130, 142, 147, 179, 183–
    189, 198, 206, 211
*Browning, Introduction to the Study
    of*, 56, 60, 61
Browning, Oscar, 145 *n.*
Browning, Robert :
    Carlyle's appreciation of, 31, 32
    Christianity, attitude to, 25–26,
        29–30, 76, 84–85, 188, 190
    Critics, attitude to, 69, 70, 74,
        77–82, 130–136
    Dramatic quality of poetry, 83,
        136, 183 f.

Erudition, 83
Family origins, 69, 115
Individualism, 170–174, 180
Love, philosophy of, 33, 86,
    122–123, 159, 175, 205
Obscurity, 26–27, 31, 52–53,
    56, 66, 67, 71, 104, 119, 134–
    135, 192, 207
Optimism, 49–50, 57, 62, 92–
    94, 115–118, 125
Outward appearance, 129, 139 f.
Poems. *See* Index II.
Poetical technique, 25, 26, 27,
    31, 61, 113, 118
Practical common sense, 141,
    142, 144
Psychological insight, 31, 52, 58,
    66, 123–124
Romantic element in, 121–123,
    125
Ruskin's appreciation of, 32,
    133, 134
Social functions, love of, 142,
    143
Browning Encyclopædia, A, 70
Browning for Beginners, 92
Browning Society (of London), 11,
    56, 58, 67, 91, 133, 134
Burdett, Osbert, 92
Bury, Professor, 68
Butler, Samuel, 94 *n.*

Carlyle, 31, 32, 35
Celtic School of Poets, 43–45, 47,
    56
Celtic Twilight, The, 43
Century Magazine, The, 132
Chambers, Robert, 19
Chapman, Swinburne's essay on,
    51, 58
Childe Harold, 26
Chesterton, G. K., 16, 90, 170
Christian Remembrancer, The, 28
Collingwood, W. G., 133
Colvin, Sir Sidney, 147, 197
Crashaw, 121

Dante, 138

215

INDEX (II)

WORKS OF BROWNING MENTIONED OR QUOTED IN THE TEXT